CONTENTS

4   Internet links
6   How we know about the Romans
8   The town of Pompeii

EARLY ROME

10   The founding of Rome
12   The growth of Rome
14   The last king of Rome

THE ROMAN REPUBLIC

16   The conquest of Italy
18   Masters of the Mediterranean
20   Citizens and senators
22   The Republic in crisis
24   The life of Caesar

THE ROMAN EMPIRE

26   The birth of the Empire
28   Emperors of Rome
30   The city of Rome
32   The Roman army
34   A soldier's life
36   Expanding the Empire
38   Running the Empire
40   Travel and trade
42   Crime and punishment

EVERYDAY LIFE

44   Family life
46   Growing up
48   Roman women
49   Slaves and freedmen
50   Living in a town
52   A house in town
54   Living in the country

56   A country villa
58   Food and cooking
60   At a dinner party
62   Fashion and beauty
64   At the baths
66   At the Games
68   At the races
70   Plays and pantomimes
72   Gods and goddesses
74   Beliefs and superstitions
76   Healing the sick
78   Crafts and trades
80   Builders and engineers
82   Amazing architecture
84   Painting and sculpture
86   Magnificent mosaics

THE END OF THE EMPIRE

88   The Empire weakens
90   The rise of Christianity
92   Barbarians and Byzantines
94   The legacy of Rome
96   Lasting Latin

FACTFINDER

98   More about the Empire
100   The organization of the army
102   Gods, goddesses and festivals
104   Legends of Rome
106   Dates, time and numbers
108   Money and banking
109   Roman law
110   What's new?
112   Who's who in the Roman world
116   Time chart
120   Glossary
122   Index
128   Acknowledgements

INTERNET LINKS

Throughout this book we have suggested interesting websites where you can find out more about the Roman world. You'll find descriptions of the recommended websites in the Internet Links boxes on the pages of this book, and there are links to all the websites at the Usborne Quicklinks Website.

USBORNE QUICKLINKS

To visit the websites, follow these simple instructions to go to the Usborne Quicklinks Website.

1. Go to **www.usborne-quicklinks.com**

2. Type the keywords for this book: **roman world**

3. Type the page number of the links you want to visit.

4. Click on the links to go to the websites.

Here are some of the things you can do on the websites recommended in this book:

- Play the role of a Roman emperor in an online game.

- Take a virtual tour of a fort on Hadrian's Wall or explore the Colosseum in Rome.

- Try your hand as a Roman engineer and design an aqueduct.

- Watch video re-enactments of Roman soldiers preparing for battle and command a Roman legion.

A statue of Apollo, the Roman god of the Sun, music, prophecy and healing

INTERNET SAFETY

Ask your parent's or guardian's permission before you connect to the Internet and make sure you follow these simple rules:

- Never give out information about yourself, such as your real name, address, phone number or the name of your school.

- If a site asks you to log in or register by typing your name or email address, ask permission from an adult first.

Please read and follow the Internet safety guidelines on the Usborne Quicklinks Website.

NOTE FOR PARENTS

The websites described in this book are regularly reviewed, but the content of a website may change at any time and Usborne Publishing is not responsible for the content on any website other than its own.

We recommend that children are supervised while on the Internet. Please ensure that your children read and follow the safety guidelines printed above. For more information, see the Net Help area on the Usborne Quicklinks Website.

Realplayer® is a registered trademark of RealNetworks, Inc.

Windows Media® player is a registered trademark of Microsoft Corporation in the United States and/or other countries.

Flash® is the trademark of Macromedia, Inc.

SITE AVAILABILITY

The links in Usborne Quicklinks are regularly reviewed and updated, but occasionally you may get a message that a site is unavailable. This might be temporary, so try again later, or even the next day. If a website closes down, we will replace it with a new link. Sometimes we add extra links too, so when you visit Usborne Quicklinks, the links may be slightly different from those described in your book.

WHAT YOU NEED

To visit the websites you need a computer with an Internet connection and a web browser (the software that lets you look at information on the Internet).

To view video clips and animations and listen to sounds, you may need small, free programs called 'plug-ins'. For example, to watch video clips and listen to sounds, you need Windows Media® player or Realplayer® . For playing animations you need a plug-in called 'Flash'.

If you go to a website and do not have the necessary plug-in, a message will come up on the screen. There is usually a link to click on to download the plug-in.

For more information about plug-ins, go to the Usborne Quicklinks Website and click on 'Net Help'.

INTERNET HELP

For help using the Internet and Usborne Quicklinks, go to the Net Help area on the Usborne Quicklinks Website. There you will find links and information on how to keep your computer up to date, and tips on how to browse the Internet safely and securely.

You will also find links to download the free 'plug-in' programs you may need to play sounds or video clips (see left). There are step-by-step instructions for installing and setting up the plug-ins, and advice on downloading pictures from the Internet and using them in your schoolwork.

For more help on using your web browser and the Internet, click on 'Help' in the menu at the top of your web browser. There you will find a huge, searchable database of information.

COMPUTER VIRUSES

A computer virus is a small program that can seriously damage your computer. A virus can get into your computer when you download programs from the Internet, or in an attachment that arrives with an email.

We strongly recommend that you buy anti-virus software to protect your computer, and that you update the anti-virus software regularly to guard your computer against new viruses.

To find out more about viruses, go to the Net Help area on the Usborne Quicklinks Website.

HOW WE KNOW ABOUT THE ROMANS

Although Roman civilization began well over 2,500 years ago, we have plenty of information about how the Romans lived. The works of Roman writers can still be read today, hundreds of buildings survive from Roman times, and objects and ruins that once lay buried underground have been uncovered by experts, known as archaeologists.

RESCUED WRITING

Very few original Roman texts survive, but in the late Empire, Christian monks began copying out Latin manuscripts. Thanks to these copies, we can learn a great deal about the way the Romans lived and thought.

Writers such as Livy, Tacitus and Suetonius provide a vivid record of Roman history. Poets, like Virgil and Ovid, bring Roman legends to life. Pliny's letters offer insights into daily life, and the biting attacks of Martial and Juvenal reveal the shocking side of Roman society.

ROMAN REMAINS

The Romans were such skilled builders that many of their temples, arenas and bridges are still standing today. Archaeologists study these buildings, along with hundreds more that are now in ruins or have been buried underground.

From the remains of Roman buildings, experts can learn about ancient art, architecture, engineering and town planning. They can also build up a picture of how the Romans lived in their cities and homes.

Here you can see part of the forum in the Roman town of Sbeitla, in Tunisia.

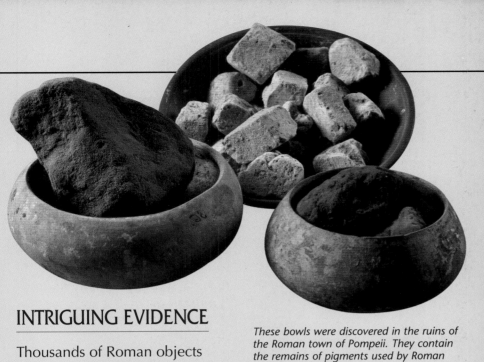

INTRIGUING EVIDENCE

Thousands of Roman objects have been found in ruined buildings, rescued from shipwrecks, or even dug up in flowerbeds. These objects range from basic pots and tools to elaborate goblets and necklaces, and all of them help to create a detailed impression of Roman life.

These bowls were discovered in the ruins of the Roman town of Pompeii. They contain the remains of pigments used by Roman artists to paint frescoes.

A Roman mosaic showing a gladiator

By studying Roman graves, archaeologists can discover how long people lived and the diseases they suffered from. Graffiti scratched on ancient walls reveals the views of ordinary Roman citizens, while cargo discovered in shipwrecks gives a clear idea of the kinds of goods that merchants traded 2,000 years ago.

Many Roman buildings contain paintings and mosaics showing scenes from everyday life. Statues portray gods, emperors and generals, while triumphal arches and columns are carved with scenes from the history of Rome.

MODERN METHODS

Archaeologists today use an amazing range of methods to help them uncover the past. Photos taken from the air reveal the outlines of buried walls, while magnetic sensors can detect structures hidden under the soil. This type of study is called a geophysical survey.

But perhaps most valuable of all is the careful analysis of plants and creatures found at archaeological sites. Experts study remains ranging in size from skeletons to pollen grains, and this painstaking work can reveal fascinating details about the kind of countryside people lived in and the food that they ate.

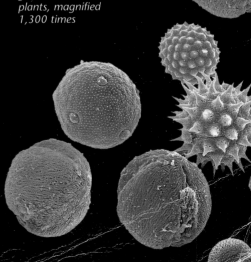

A selection of pollen grains from different plants, magnified 1,300 times

THE TOWN OF POMPEII

One of the best places to learn about the Romans is the town of Pompeii in southern Italy. In AD79, Pompeii was buried under layers of ash from a violent volcanic eruption, but the ash that buried the town also preserved it. Buildings, furniture, tools and possessions survived almost intact, clearly showing what life was like on the day disaster struck.

Many lively mosaics and paintings have been uncovered at Pompeii. This sign warned people to beware of the fierce dog.

A LIVELY TOWN

Pompeii was a thriving town close to the Bay of Naples. Its wealth came from exporting wine, olive oil and wool, and several of its citizens were rich enough to own luxurious villas. The town's busy streets were lined with workshops, inns and shops, and the townspeople relaxed by visiting public baths, watching plays, or cheering on the gladiators in the town's arena.

ERUPTION!

One clear summer's morning in AD79, a massive explosion rocked the streets of Pompeii, as nearby Mount Vesuvius erupted into life. Soon, the town was engulfed in dust, lumps of burning rock fell from the sky, buildings shook, and the streets were filled with terrified people running in all directions.

The destruction continued throughout the night and into the next day, when the writer Pliny records that the sky grew blacker than the darkest night. Many people were suffocated by hot, dusty winds, and Pompeii was gradually buried under a blanket of ash.

Here you can see how Pompeii would have looked at the time that Mount Vesuvius erupted.

REMARKABLE REMAINS

The town remained buried until the 18th century, when archaeologists began to uncover its buildings and were amazed at what they found. Statues, furniture and lamps had survived, as well as smaller objects such as dishes and rings. People who had died suddenly from suffocation had left a perfect imprint in the hardened ash - caught forever in the act of escaping, or huddled close to one another for comfort.

This plaster cast of a man was made by filling the hollow shape left by his body.

INTERNET LINKS
For links to websites where you can browse an online exhibit about Pompeii and see photo galleries of everyday life, go to **www.usborne-quicklinks.com**

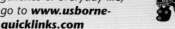

An Etruscan wall painting of a musician from a tomb at Tarquinia, near Rome

EARLY ROME

THE FOUNDING OF ROME

Around 3,000 years ago, a tribe of people known as the Latins settled on the hilltops above the banks of the Tiber, in the land that is now Italy. This cluster of small villages eventually grew to become the city of Rome - one of the most splendid cities in the ancient world and the capital of the mighty Roman Empire.

Urns like this, in the shape of a house, were used by the Latins for burying the ashes of their dead.

LAND OF THE LATINS

The Latins lived on a fertile plain on the west coast of Italy. They spoke an early form of the language now known as Latin, and the area where they lived was known as Latium. The Latins grew crops and kept animals, and around 1,000BC they began building the first small villages on the future site of Rome.

The site had lots of advantages. At just that spot the Tiber narrowed, and there was an island in the middle, making it possible for people to cross. The coast was 25km (about 15 miles) away - close enough to reach the sea by boat, but far enough away to be safe from the pirates who roamed the Mediterranean. And from the hills above the river, it was easy to spot enemies and fight them off.

The Latins lived in simple, wooden huts with thatched roofs. They built their homes on the hilltops above the Tiber and used the marshy valleys below as cemeteries for burying their dead. Gradually, these small villages spread down the hillsides and, some time during the 8th century BC, they merged to form a single town - Rome.

Here, you can see an early Latin settlement on the Palatine Hill, one of the seven hills which later became the site of Rome.

INTERNET LINKS
For links to websites where you can read more about the founding of Rome and the legend of Romulus and Remus, go to www.usborne-quicklinks.com

A wooden fence helped to protect the village from enemies.

The marshy valley below the Palatine became a meeting place for people from the surrounding villages.

MYTHS AND LEGENDS

Much later, Roman historians, such as Livy, combined a Greek myth and a Roman folktale to provide a far grander account of how their great city was founded.

The story began with Aeneas - a mythical hero from Greek legend who had escaped from the conquered city of Troy. After many adventures, Aeneas finally arrived in Italy, where he married a Latin princess and started a new line of kings.

According to Roman tradition, two of Aeneas's descendants were twin boys named Romulus and Remus. They were said to be the sons of Mars, the god of war. The twins' great-uncle, Amulius, wanted them out of the way and ordered them to be drowned in the Tiber. But Amulius's men took pity on the babies and set them afloat in a cradle. They drifted ashore where they were found by a she-wolf, who fed them until they were rescued by a kindly shepherd.

A later Roman coin showing a portrait of Romulus

When the boys grew up, they killed their wicked great-uncle and decided to build a new city on the banks of the Tiber. But as the city walls were being built, Remus mocked his brother, and they had a violent argument. Romulus killed Remus and became king of the new city, which was named "Rome" after him. According to tradition, this happened in 753BC.

A bronze statue of the she-wolf feeding Romulus and Remus

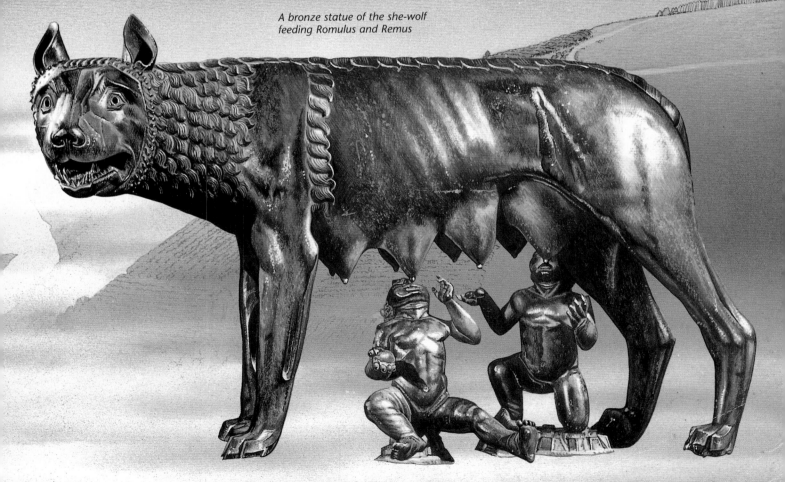

THE GROWTH OF ROME

In the 8th century BC, while Rome was growing into a city, the Latins were just one of many groups of people who lived on the Italian peninsula. To the north lay the great Etruscan civilization, while the south was dominated by the Greeks who had set up colonies there. In between were numerous tribes of hill-farmers, such as the Sabines. All these people had a part to play in the history of Rome.

THE SABINE WOMEN

According to the Roman historian Livy, the newly founded city of Rome suffered from a shortage of women. So the Latins invited the nearby Sabines to take part in a festival of games, and then kidnapped all their daughters. Although the story is unlikely to be true, some of the early inhabitants of Rome were Sabines, and the legend may have grown up to explain how they came to be there.

Map showing some of the different groups of people who lived in Italy

GREAT GREECE

As early as 750BC, Greek colonists began setting up cities in southern Italy and on the coast of Sicily. The Greeks had such a strong influence in this area that the Romans later called it *Magna Graecia* - or "Great Greece".

As well as bringing goods to trade - such as fine pottery, metalwork and wine - the Greeks also brought with them their science, literature, drama, art and architecture. All of these had a huge effect on Roman culture.

The ruins of a typical Greek temple, built by Greek colonists at Segesta, on the island of Sicily

THE ETRUSCANS

The people who had the greatest influence on early Rome were the Etruscans, who controlled the area north of the Tiber. No one is quite sure where the Etruscans came from. Some experts think they were native to Italy, while others think they came from the eastern Mediterranean. Their civilization, based on a group of large, well-planned cities, was at its peak between 800BC and 400BC.

A gold perfume bottle, found in the tomb of an Etruscan nobleman

The Etruscans traded with the Greeks in southern Italy, and adopted the Greek alphabet, which they passed on to the Romans. They were highly skilled artists, who created elaborate sculptures in bronze and terracotta, and decorated the walls of their tombs with brightly painted frescoes.

Many of the things we think of as typically Roman were inherited from the Etruscans. They enjoyed chariot races and gladiator fights, built arches, aqueducts and sewers, and invented the toga. They also played a part in the early government of Rome.

THE KINGS OF ROME

Early Rome was ruled by a king, who was chosen and advised by a council of elders - or *senes*. According to Roman tradition, there was a series of seven kings, but there are no written records from the time to back this up. The last three kings were said to be Etruscans.

Rome was situated on a route used by Etruscan traders to cross the Tiber, and experts believe that around 600BC the Etruscans took control of the city. Under the Etruscans, Rome grew into an impressive city with a public square surrounded by temples, a proper drainage system and huge defensive walls.

INTERNET LINKS
For links to websites where you can watch short movie clips about the Etruscans and the growth of the city of Rome, go to **www.usborne-quicklinks.com**

The Etruscans often decorated the lids of their coffins with terracotta sculptures, such as this one of a man and his wife.

THE LAST KING OF ROME

The Romans resented the Etruscan kings who ruled over them, and the last king - Tarquinius Superbus, or "Tarquin the Proud" - was particularly unpopular. His story is told by the Roman historian Livy, who was writing 500 years later, and it is probably based on folktales handed down by generations of Romans.

A REIGN OF TERROR

Tarquin became ruler after murdering the previous king by throwing him down the steps of the Senate House. He was a ruthless tyrant, who ruled without consulting the council and who put to death anyone he pleased.

Late one night, Tarquin's son brutally attacked a Roman noblewoman named Lucretia, while her husband was away. This was the final straw for the Romans. Outraged, they drove Tarquin and his family out of the city.

HORATIO THE HERO

Tarquin appealed to the Etruscans for help, and finally persuaded the king of Clusium (an Etruscan city farther north) to attack Rome. But to reach the city, the Etruscan army first had to cross a wooden bridge over the Tiber.

A fearless Roman soldier named Horatio held the Etruscans back, while the Romans destroyed the bridge behind him. Horatio then jumped into the river and swam back to his friends - Rome was saved.

Here you can see Horatio defending the bridge against the Etruscan army.

THE BIRTH OF THE REPUBLIC

Although all these stories are legend, rather than fact, the Romans did eventually drive out their Etruscan rulers. The reign of the last king ended in 510BC or 509BC, and Rome became an independent republic.

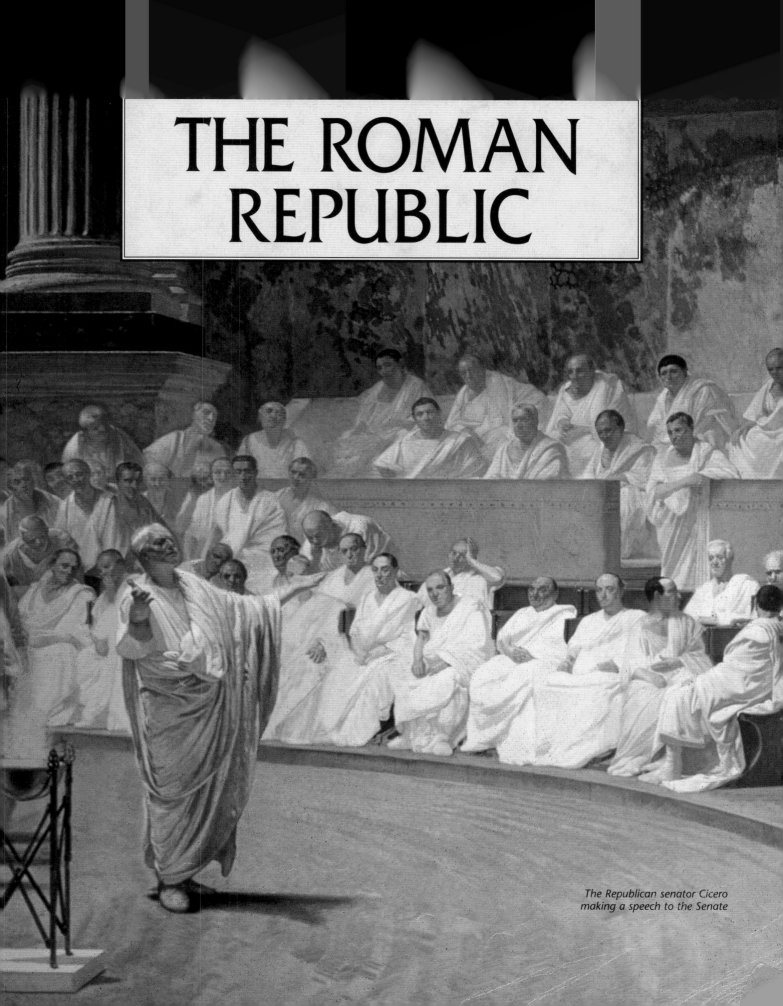

THE ROMAN REPUBLIC

The Republican senator Cicero making a speech to the Senate

THE CONQUEST OF ITALY

The early Roman Republic was surrounded on all sides by enemies. To the north were the powerful Etruscans, while central Italy was swarming with fierce mountain tribes, such as the Volsci, the Aequi and the Samnites. At times, Rome was also at war with rival Latin cities nearby. By using a mixture of military power and clever politics, the Romans gradually fought off their enemies and took over their land.

Map of Roman lands in 264BC

Here you can see an army of Gauls climbing the Capitol Hill to attack Rome at night.

Roman soldiers, woken by the cackling of geese, rushed to defend the Capitol.

GETTING STARTED

At first, the Republic wasn't strong enough to defeat the mountain tribes by itself and was forced to accept the help of a group of Latin cities, known as the Latin League. By 400BC, Rome was the leading city in the League, and the Republic had doubled in size. Soon, the Romans began expanding to the north as well, defeating the nearby Etruscan city of Veii in 396BC.

ROME UNDER ATTACK

Then, disaster struck. An army of Gauls - a Celtic tribe from central Europe - swept south through Italy and defeated the Romans in a fierce battle at the Allia river. In 390BC, the Gauls attacked Rome, burned most of its buildings to the ground, and besieged the Capitol Hill - the religious heart of the city.

According to legend, the Gauls tried to creep up on the Capitol late one night, but they disturbed some geese that were kept at one of the temples. The cackling geese woke the Romans just in time to fight off the attack. The Capitol was besieged for seven months, and when the Gauls eventually moved away, they left the city in ruins.

BACK ON TRACK

Gradually, the Romans rebuilt their city and began to win back the land they had lost. The other cities in the Latin League resented Rome's increasing power, and war broke out. In 338BC, Rome defeated the League and took control of Latium.

At the same time, Rome was involved in three wars against a hill tribe called the Samnites. The Samnites won several spectacular victories, but were eventually defeated - along with their allies the Gauls and the Etruscans. By 290BC, Rome controlled most of central and northern Italy.

The Gauls were fierce warriors, who fought with swords and spears.

This fresco shows two Samnite warriors wearing helmets decorated with feathers.

KEEPING CONTROL

The Romans could be very generous to people they conquered. Any city that surrendered quickly was offered an alliance, and its people were given some of the privileges of Roman citizens. But those who resisted were brutally killed or sold as slaves. These tactics helped the Romans keep their growing lands under control.

THE PYRRHIC WARS

In 282BC, Rome was drawn into a dispute between rival Greek cities in the south, and agreed to help defend the city of Thurii. But Tarentum - another Greek city nearby - was suspicious of Rome's motives, and appealed to a Greek king named Pyrrhus for help. In the war that followed, Pyrrhus defeated the Romans twice, but lost vast numbers of his own soldiers, remarking grimly: "Another victory like that, and I'll be ruined."

Pyrrhus was eventually defeated in 275BC, and by 264BC the Romans dominated all of Italy. Rome was now one of the most powerful states in the Mediterranean.

This is a statue of King Pyrrhus. The phrase "a Pyrrhic victory" is still used today when the cost of winning is too high.

MASTERS OF THE MEDITERRANEAN

While Rome was gaining control of Italy, the western Mediterranean was dominated by the great trading empire of Carthage, on the coast of North Africa. As long as they weren't competing for trade, the Romans and the Carthaginians left each other in peace. But in 264BC, a series of bitter wars broke out between them. These wars - called the Punic Wars - would eventually decide who ruled the Mediterranean.

Coin showing Hamilcar Barca, who led the Carthaginian army during the First Punic War

ALL AT SEA

The First Punic War began when both Rome and Carthage stepped in to sort out a dispute on the island of Sicily, off the coast of Italy.

To win the war, Rome would have to defeat the powerful Carthaginian navy, but the Romans had very few ships and no experience of fighting at sea. Luckily, they found a stranded Carthaginian warship and used it as a model to build a fleet of their own.

The Romans added a spiked drawbridge - called a corvus - to their ships. Here, you can see it being used to board a Carthaginian ship.

The Romans won two early sea battles - but twice lost all their ships in violent storms. Having rebuilt their fleet, they finally defeated the Carthaginians in 241BC. Carthage was forced to pay a huge fine and also agreed to let Rome have control of Sicily - its first overseas territory. The Romans later seized Sardinia and Corsica as well.

HANDLING HANNIBAL

In search of a new empire, the Carthaginians invaded Spain. In 219BC, they attacked the Spanish city of Saguntum - an ally of Rome - provoking the Second Punic War. The next year, the Carthaginian general, Hannibal, set off with 35,000 men and 37 elephants to invade Italy.

When the corvus was dropped onto the enemy's ship, Roman soldiers could charge across.

Hannibal led his troops across the Pyrenees and the Alps - losing 10,000 men and all but one of the elephants on the way. But he was an outstanding general, and his men won battle after battle. At Cannae in 216BC they wiped out an entire Roman army, one of the worst defeats suffered by Rome.

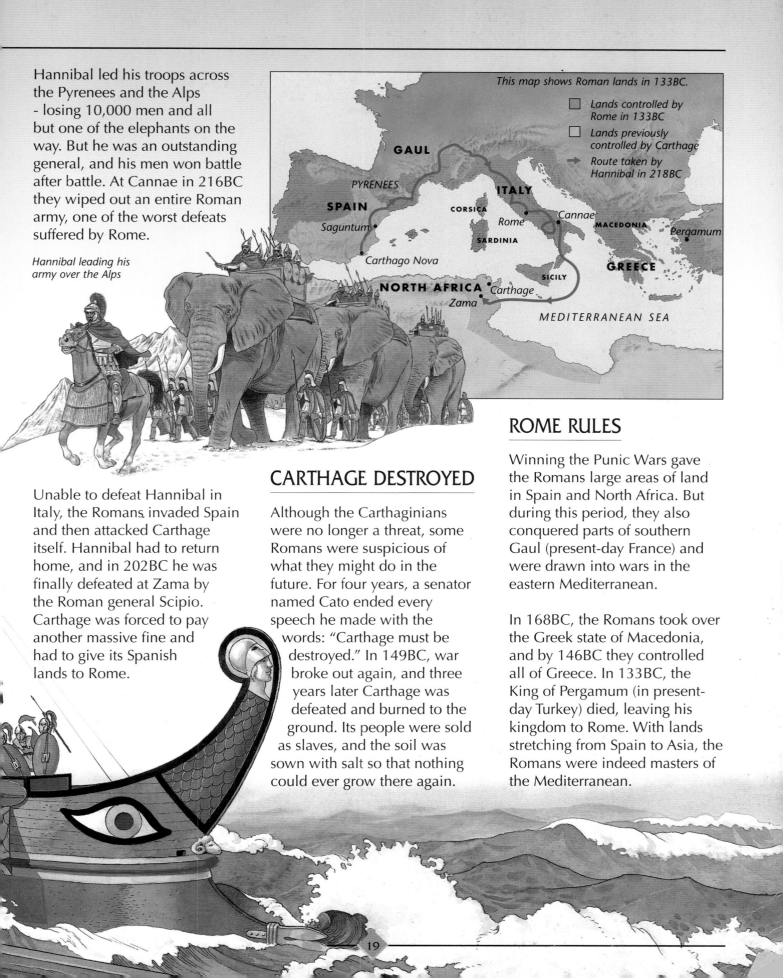

Hannibal leading his army over the Alps

This map shows Roman lands in 133BC.

☐ Lands controlled by Rome in 133BC

☐ Lands previously controlled by Carthage

→ Route taken by Hannibal in 218BC

GAUL

PYRENEES

SPAIN

Saguntum

Carthago Nova

NORTH AFRICA

Zama

Carthage

CORSICA

Rome

SARDINIA

ITALY

Cannae

SICILY

MACEDONIA

Pergamum

GREECE

MEDITERRANEAN SEA

Unable to defeat Hannibal in Italy, the Romans invaded Spain and then attacked Carthage itself. Hannibal had to return home, and in 202BC he was finally defeated at Zama by the Roman general Scipio. Carthage was forced to pay another massive fine and had to give its Spanish lands to Rome.

CARTHAGE DESTROYED

Although the Carthaginians were no longer a threat, some Romans were suspicious of what they might do in the future. For four years, a senator named Cato ended every speech he made with the words: "Carthage must be destroyed." In 149BC, war broke out again, and three years later Carthage was defeated and burned to the ground. Its people were sold as slaves, and the soil was sown with salt so that nothing could ever grow there again.

ROME RULES

Winning the Punic Wars gave the Romans large areas of land in Spain and North Africa. But during this period, they also conquered parts of southern Gaul (present-day France) and were drawn into wars in the eastern Mediterranean.

In 168BC, the Romans took over the Greek state of Macedonia, and by 146BC they controlled all of Greece. In 133BC, the King of Pergamum (in present-day Turkey) died, leaving his kingdom to Rome. With lands stretching from Spain to Asia, the Romans were indeed masters of the Mediterranean.

CITIZENS AND SENATORS

As far as the Romans were concerned, there were two kinds of people - citizens and non-citizens. Citizens had special rights and privileges, and were given extra protection under the law, so citizenship was highly prized. But in return, all citizens were expected to serve Rome by voting in elections, fighting in the army, and perhaps working for the government.

CITIZENS AND NON-CITIZENS

Originally, citizens had to be born in Rome and have parents who were Roman citizens. Most were farmers or craftsmen. Non-citizens included provincials (who lived outside Rome but within Roman territory), slaves, and foreigners (who lived outside Roman territory). Provincials couldn't vote in elections, and, unlike citizens, they paid taxes. Slaves were owned by other people and didn't have any rights at all.

Roman women, like the one shown here with her slave, weren't classed as full citizens and weren't allowed to vote.

PATRICIANS AND PLEBEIANS

Roman citizens were divided into two groups - patricians and plebeians. In early Rome, the heads of the richest and most powerful families were known as *patres* - or "fathers". The patricians were descended from these men and they were the leading citizens in Rome.

A statue of a patrician holding busts of two of his ancestors

Everyone who wasn't a patrician was classed as a plebeian. Many plebeians had no land or skills and were extremely poor. Others were shopkeepers or craftworkers, while one group - known as *equites* - were bankers or merchants. These wealthy men were descended from the first Roman cavalry officers.

RICH RULERS

During the Republic, Rome was ruled by the Senate - a group of 300 men drawn from important patrician families. To qualify for the Senate, a man had to own a vast amount of land, but once appointed he held the job for life. Senators were expected to spend lots of money on entertaining, providing for their supporters and paying for public buildings, and some senators ended up bankrupt.

A coin showing the Senate House in Rome

TOP JOBS

After being consul, a man could become a proconsul and govern one of the Roman provinces abroad. Another important job was done by the two censors, who made sure there were enough senators and checked that anyone claiming to be a Roman citizen genuinely was one. In dire emergencies, the Senate sometimes appointed one man to be dictator for a time. He had absolute authority over everyone else.

The fasces - an axe tied to a bundle of rods - was the symbol of a consul's power.

POWER TO THE PLEBS

Very early in Rome's history, the plebeians - especially the wealthy ones - began to resent the patricians' power and wanted a share in governing the city. In 494BC, the plebeians actually threatened to leave Rome and start a city of their own. So the Senate agreed that the plebeians could set up their own council, and elect officials - called tribunes - to protect their interests.

In 450BC, after riots by the plebeians, a list of laws known as the Twelve Tables was drawn up and displayed in the Forum. This meant that everyone knew what the laws were and could check if the judges were following them.

Over the years, plebeians won the right to become senators and stand for government positions. The first plebeian consul was elected in 366BC, and after 287BC all decisions of the Plebeian Council had to become law - even if the Senate didn't agree.

THE CAREER LADDER

For a young Roman who wanted a career in politics, the road to the top was long, difficult and expensive. After spending a few years in the army, the budding politician had to get himself elected to a series of government positions. The most senior position was that of consul. The pictures on the right show the usual career path for an ambitious Roman.

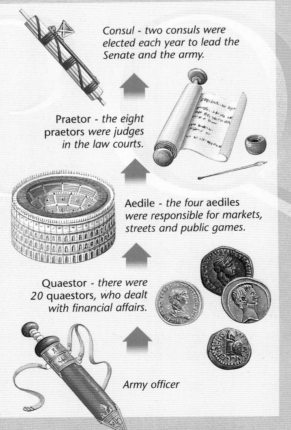

Consul - two consuls were elected each year to lead the Senate and the army.

Praetor - the eight praetors were judges in the law courts.

Aedile - the four aediles were responsible for markets, streets and public games.

Quaestor - there were 20 quaestors, who dealt with financial affairs.

Army officer

SPQR

*These letters stand for **S**enatus **P**opulus**q**ue **R**omanus (the Senate and people of Rome). They are often found on Roman carvings.*

THE REPUBLIC IN CRISIS

By the 3rd century BC, the plebeians were playing a much bigger part in the government of Rome. Some patrician senators began to feel threatened, and tensions grew. From the 2nd century BC, one crisis followed another, plunging the Republic into a period of turmoil and bloodshed.

Great Roman generals were given a parade - or triumph - to celebrate their victories. This scene shows a typical triumph.

LAND MATTERS

As Rome began building its empire, many men were too busy fighting overseas in the army to farm their own land. The farms fell into disrepair, and many were bought up by rich landowners.

Without land or jobs, country people drifted into Rome, where they remained very poor. Since only landowners fought in the army, there was soon a shortage of soldiers too.

In 133BC, a tribune named Tiberius Gracchus suggested that any land that had been seized by the rich should be given to poor city dwellers.

Soldiers wearing laurel wreaths shouted, "Io triomphe!" (behold the triumph).

But many senators were opposed to this, because they owned a lot of the land. Riots broke out, and Tiberius was murdered. In 123BC, Tiberius' brother Gaius was elected tribune. He, too, planned to help the poor, but was also mercilessly killed.

With the government in crisis, two opposing groups emerged in the Senate - the Populares, who were in favour of making reforms, and the Boni, who didn't want to make any changes at all.

A slave held a laurel wreath over the general's head. It was his job to repeat in the general's ear, "Remember, you are just a man."

The general rode in a golden chariot. His face was painted red and he carried an olive branch.

MARIUS AND THE ARMY

In 107BC, one of Rome's greatest generals - Gaius Marius - won a war in North Africa, and became a national hero when he also defeated some tribes from Gaul. But he wasn't so skilled at politics, and he angered many senators by supporting reform.

As consul, Marius radically reorganized the army, allowing all citizens to enlist. These new soldiers were very poor, and relied on their generals to get them land grants when they retired. Soldiers were paid a wage, and given equipment. This accidentally resulted in a dramatic change in politics, as successful generals found they could use their devoted armies to win power for themselves, and to settle political differences.

MURDER AND MAYHEM

In 88BC, Cornelius Sulla became consul and was asked to lead an army against the King of Pontus (now part of Turkey). Marius thought he should have been chosen instead and he challenged Sulla. Sulla promptly marched his army to Rome, took control of the city and drove Marius out.

Sulla then set off for Pontus. As soon as he'd gone, Marius reappeared with an army of his own, took over the city and put Sulla's supporters to death. Marius died in 86BC, but when Sulla returned to Rome he found Marius's men still in charge. He had all of them killed and ruled Rome as dictator from 82BC to 80BC.

POMPEY THE GREAT

One of the generals who had served under Sulla's command was Gnaeus Pompeius, known as Pompey the Great. Pompey won victories in Spain in 72BC and helped the senator Crassus to crush a slave rebellion led by a gladiator named Spartacus. In 70BC, he and Crassus became consuls.

A sculpture of Pompey the Great

Soon, Pompey was a hero. In just three months, he cleared the whole of the Mediterranean of pirates. He then reorganized Rome's lands in the Middle East and conquered large areas of new territory. But when he returned to Rome, the Senate refused to support what he had done. Frustrated, Pompey looked for new allies - one of these was a talented politician named Gaius Julius Caesar.

Prisoners of war were displayed on a platform, along with their weapons.

White oxen were sacrificed when the procession reached the temple of Jupiter, on the Capitol Hill.

Treasures captured in battle

The procession was led by senators.

THE LIFE OF CAESAR

Gaius Julius Caesar came from an old patrician family which claimed to be descended from the goddess Venus and the legendary hero Aeneas. He was a skilled politician, a talented public speaker and an outstanding general. Today, he is regarded as one of the most remarkable figures in Roman history.

A coin showing Julius Caesar

A RISING STAR

In 60BC, Caesar formed an alliance with Pompey and Crassus, and with their support he became consul the following year. After his year in office, he persuaded the Senate to give him command of Rome's lands in southern Gaul. This gave him a chance to prove himself, and soon he conquered the rest of Gaul, extending Roman territory as far as the English Channel. His popularity in Rome soared.

TROUBLE AHEAD

After the death of Caesar's daughter Julia, who was married to Pompey, the bond between the two men began to weaken. Afraid of Caesar's growing power, the Senate decided to support Pompey and turn the two men against each other. Caesar was ordered to give up his command in Gaul and return home without his army. If he refused, it would mean war.

TRIUMPH AND DISASTER

In January 49BC, Caesar defied the Senate and led his army across the Rubicon river into Italy. Pompey retreated to Greece, and Caesar took control of Rome. He defeated Pompey in 48BC and then crushed rebellions in North Africa and Spain. By 45BC, Caesar was the most powerful leader Rome had ever known.

Once in power, Caesar passed new laws to help the poor and improve the way Rome's lands were run. But he took decisions without consulting the Senate, and in 44BC he became dictator for life. Some politicians were worried that he had grown too powerful, and on March 15, 44BC, a group of senators stabbed him to death. Soon after, a civil war broke out which would finally bring the Republic to an end.

A scene showing the murder of Caesar, from a modern production of Shakespeare's play Julius Caesar

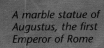

A marble statue of Augustus, the first Emperor of Rome

THE ROMAN EMPIRE

Internet link *For a link to a website where you can find out about the life of Augustus and the growing Roman Empire, go to* **www.usborne-quicklinks.com**

THE BIRTH OF THE EMPIRE

After Julius Caesar's murder in 44BC, his friend Mark Antony seemed poised to become the next Roman ruler. Caesar's adopted son and heir, Octavian, was only 18, and most people assumed he was too young to take power. But when Octavian heard of Caesar's death, he rushed to Rome, where he was welcomed by many of Caesar's supporters. Soon, a chaotic struggle for power began.

A Roman coin showing a portrait of Antony

EARLY BATTLES

Mark Antony had many enemies in the Senate, and they persuaded the other senators to declare him an outlaw in order to stop him from gaining power. With the Senate's support, Octavian led an army against Antony and defeated him at Mutina, in northern Italy.

Octavian then demanded to be made a consul, but the Senate refused, so he changed his plans. He joined forces with Antony and Lepidus - Antony's ally - and the three men stormed into Rome with a huge army. They forced the Senate to accept them as rulers, and executed thousands of their opponents. Lepidus soon retired, leaving Octavian and Antony in charge.

THE TWO RULERS

By 42BC, Antony and Octavian had gained enough power to rule. In a bid for political unity, Antony married Octavian's sister, Octavia. But Antony and Octavian argued so much that they decided to divide up Rome's territory - with Octavian ruling the west, and Antony taking the east.

☐ Octavian's territory
☐ Antony's territory

This map shows how Antony and Octavian divided up Rome's lands.

Many of Antony's ships were sunk.

The two sides tried to destroy each other's boats with metal rams.

This carving shows the Egyptian queen Cleopatra wearing a royal headdress.

Abandoning Octavia, Antony moved to Egypt where he lived for ten years with his lover, Cleopatra, the Egyptian queen. Meanwhile, Octavian stayed in Rome, and made himself popular with the Senate and the people. The two rulers became more and more suspicious of each other, and the situation grew tense.

In 31BC, war finally broke out. Octavian defeated Antony and Cleopatra in the sea battle of Actium, off the western coast of Greece, and the despairing lovers fled back to Egypt. When Octavian pursued them there, they both committed suicide.

This scene shows part of the Battle of Actium.

Octavian had more ships than Antony, and used them to surround his opponent's fleet.

HAIL AUGUSTUS!

Octavian seized control of Egypt and became sole ruler of all the Roman lands. In 27BC, he offered to let the Senate take over, but this was just for show. Octavian was supported by the army, and everyone knew that only he could unite the Roman people. The Senate gave Octavian the new name Augustus, which means "deeply respected one", and he gradually gained total control over the Roman world.

The Romans called Augustus by the military title *imperator*, from which we get the word "emperor". He is usually regarded as the first Emperor of Rome, and the period of Roman history that began with his rule is known as the Empire.

Augustus ruled wisely and efficiently, bringing peace after decades of civil war. By the time he died in AD14, most people had accepted the idea of being governed by a single powerful ruler. The Republic was over forever.

A statue of Augustus wearing the uniform of a Roman general

Catapult

EMPERORS OF ROME

Augustus was the first in a series of emperors who ruled the Roman world for over 400 years. Most emperors made a show of consulting the Senate, but in fact they ruled exactly as they pleased. Even though the emperor controlled a huge empire, his life could be in danger if he became unpopular. Jealous rivals and assassins were never far away.

This coin shows the Emperor Tiberius wearing a laurel crown - a symbol of military victory often worn by Roman emperors.

BRUTAL BODYGUARDS

The emperor had a special group of soldiers called the Praetorian Guard, whose job was to protect him and his family. However, these supposedly loyal bodyguards sometimes had their own ideas about who should rule Rome, and several emperors were murdered by their protectors.

MAD, BAD AND DANGEROUS TO KNOW

After Augustus's death in AD14, the imperial family was plunged into a turbulent time of scheming and betrayal, and some of the emperors from this period behaved extremely cruelly.

Augustus's step-son, the Emperor Tiberius (AD14-37), was a ruthless and corrupt man. Worried that people were plotting to assassinate him, he executed dozens of important Romans and fled to the island of Capri. He stayed there for the last 11 years of his rule, and any visitor he didn't like was thrown over the cliffs to his death.

The next emperor, Caligula (AD37-41), may have been insane. He believed he was a god, and it was said that he tried to have his horse elected consul. He once made his soldiers attack the sea, because he was angry with the sea god Neptune.

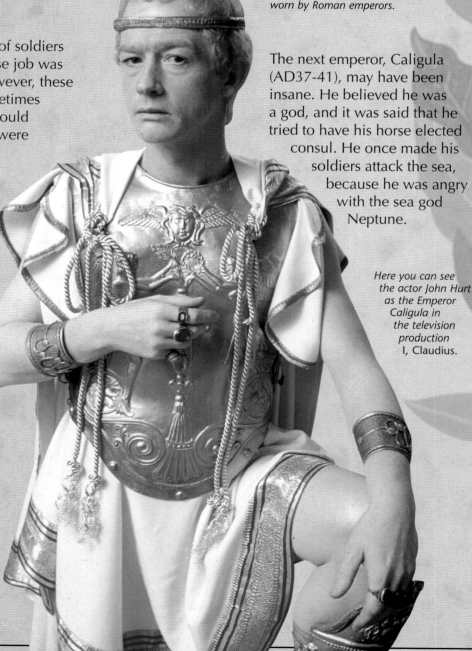

Here you can see the actor John Hurt as the Emperor Caligula in the television production I, Claudius.

The Emperor Nero, who was thought by many to have started the Great Fire of Rome

The Emperor Nero (AD54-68) was viciously cruel, and had his wife and mother murdered, as well as anyone who dared to oppose him. He also loved art, music and poetry, and shocked his people by playing the lyre and singing in public. (Musicians weren't considered respectable.) Nero's performances could be very long, and the audience was forbidden to leave before the end. Sometimes, people pretended to be dead so that they could be carried out.

THE YEAR OF THE FOUR EMPERORS

After Nero's death came a period of incredible turmoil. In AD69, Rome was ruled by no fewer than four emperors within a single year. The last of these emperors, Vespasian, was a general in the Roman army. With the support of his soldiers, he finally brought stability back to the Empire.

REASONABLE RULERS

Many emperors were sensible, fair rulers who did their best to keep an enormous empire running smoothly.

Tiberius's nephew Claudius (AD41-54) had been left crippled by a childhood disease, and most people thought he wasn't capable of ruling. In fact, he turned out to be an excellent emperor, although he was eventually murdered. Some historians think his wife gave him poisoned mushrooms to eat.

The Emperor Claudius was a shy and nervous man, but an efficient ruler. He conquered Britain in AD43.

In AD96, Nerva became emperor, and ruled wisely and fairly. After him came four capable emperors, and together these rulers are known as the five good emperors. They expanded the Empire, improved its organization, and won the support of senators by treating the Senate with respect.

PASSING ON POWER

At first, a man could only become emperor if he was related to the last ruler. But Nerva started a new tradition, when he chose and adopted the man he wanted to rule after him. (See page 99 for a full list of Roman emperors.)

INTERNET LINKS
For links to websites where you can search an encyclopedia of Roman emperors and play the role of Emperor in an online game, go to www.usborne-quicklinks.com

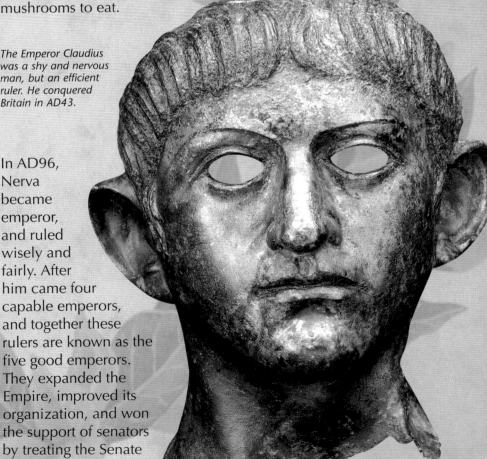

THE CITY OF ROME

Ancient Rome - capital of the Empire and home of the Roman emperors - was a city of huge contrasts. As well as splendid public buildings, there were plenty of rickety, overcrowded apartment blocks, and while wealthy citizens enjoyed a life of incredible luxury, many Romans were desperately poor.

INTERNET LINKS
For links to websites where you can explore an interactive map of the Roman Forum, and find out more about the great fire, go to **www.usborne-quicklinks.com**

CITY OF MARBLE

Rome was constantly changing, as each emperor tried to leave his mark on the city by putting up impressive new buildings and monuments. The Emperor Augustus completely transformed Rome, boasting proudly that he had found it a city of bricks and left it a city of marble.

At the heart of the city was the Roman Forum - a large, open space used as a market square and meeting place. Around the Forum, there were basilicas - used as law courts - and grand temples. Near one end was the *Curia* - or Senate House. As Rome grew, the Roman Forum was no longer big enough for everyone to meet, so some emperors built their own larger *fora* nearby.

WALKING THE STREETS

Most streets in Rome were extremely narrow, unbearably crowded and incredibly noisy. Carts were banned from the city during daylight hours, and shopkeepers displayed their goods in the streets. The main streets were swept clean, but the smaller alleys could be ankle-deep in waste. People often threw their refuse out of the window - an added hazard for anyone passing by.

NIGHT LIFE

As soon as dusk fell, an endless stream of delivery carts began rumbling through the city. Rome had no streetlights, so at night the city was plunged into darkness. Thieves and murderers lurked on street corners, and wealthy citizens wouldn't leave home without a group of slaves to guard them. The poet Juvenal joked that it would be foolish to go out after dark without first making a will.

Here, you can see a reconstruction of the Roman Forum at the height of the Empire.

The temple of Castor and Pollux was dedicated to the twin sons of the god Jupiter.

The buildings were faced with thin slices of gleaming white marble.

The temple of Vesta, where the Vestal Virgins kept a sacred fire burning

ON THE DOLE

By the first century AD, there were over a million people living in Rome, and many of them were too poor to survive without help from the government. Rations of free grain - known as the corn dole - were handed out to the poorest 200,000 citizens and their families. Most of the grain came from Egypt, and if the grain ships were late, violent riots could break out.

FIRE! FIRE!

Most Romans lived in flimsy apartment blocks heated by metal braziers filled with burning wood. Fire was a constant danger, so Augustus organized groups of firefighters - called *vigiles* - to tackle blazes in the city. But, equipped only with buckets of water and basic hand pumps, the *vigiles* couldn't cope with the largest fires.

In AD64, Rome was devastated by the worst fire in its history. Only four of the city's fourteen districts were left undamaged, and three were burned to the ground. At the time, many Romans blamed the Emperor Nero for starting the fire so he could build himself a vast palace in the ruins of the city. Nero was said to have sung and played his lyre as he watched Rome burn, but in fact he may have tried to help put out the fires.

The temple of Jupiter on the Capitol Hill

Brightly painted statues

The Tabularium - or public record office - where state records were kept

The Basilica Julia - a court house begun by Julius Caesar and completed by Augustus

The temple of the god Saturn, who was said to have taught the Romans how to farm

Temple of Concord - or Peace

Arch of Septimius Severus

The speakers' platform - or Rostra - was used for official ceremonies, such as funeral speeches.

This is the Curia, where the Senate met.

Shrine of Venus Cloacina, goddess of the sewer

THE ROMAN ARMY

Without the mighty Roman army, the Empire could never have been created. Well-trained and highly disciplined, this formidable fighting force was one of the most feared and successful armies in history. For hundreds of years, it seemed unbeatable.

THE EARLY ARMY

In the early Republic, Rome didn't have a professional army. Only citizens who owned land were allowed to fight for Rome, and very few of these were full-time soldiers. When a war started, thousands of men were called up, but they had to provide their own weapons and equipment, and they returned home as soon as the fighting was over.

TURNING PROFESSIONAL

As the Roman army began to spend more time overseas, fighting wars to expand their territory, they needed a bigger and better army to conquer and control distant provinces. In the 2nd century BC, the army was completely transformed by a commander named Gaius Marius, who turned it into a full-time, professional fighting force.

> **INTERNET LINKS**
> For links to websites where you can watch videos of soldiers training for battle and command a Roman legion of your own, go to **www.usborne-quicklinks.com**

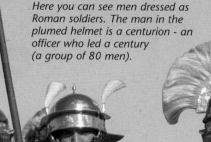

Here you can see men dressed as Roman soldiers. The man in the plumed helmet is a centurion - an officer who led a century (a group of 80 men).

Each century had a decorated staff, called a standard.

MARIUS'S MULES

Marius allowed all Roman citizens to enlist, whether they owned land or not, and each man was given the same weapons and training. Soldiers also began to receive wages, so lots of poor men joined the army. Marius made Roman soldiers carry so much heavy equipment that they became known as "Marius's mules".

ORGANIZING THE ARMY

The Roman army was divided into groups of 6,000 men, called legions. The soldiers, known as legionaries, were very well trained and highly organized.

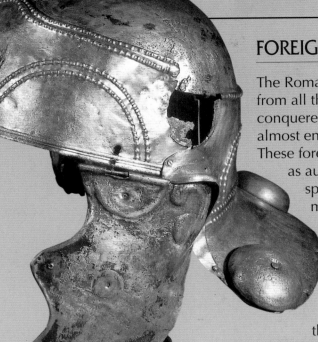

A combat helmet made of bronze and iron worn by a Roman cavalry soldier

Every legion had a gold or silver eagle that was carried by a soldier called an aquilifer, *shown in this bronze statue.*

Most soldiers fought on foot, but the army also had cavalry - mounted soldiers who rode alongside the legions and could move ahead to surround enemies. (For more about the army's organization, see pages 100 and 101.)

FOREIGN FIGHTERS

The Romans recruited soldiers from all the areas they conquered, so the army had an almost endless supply of men. These foreign warriors, known as auxiliaries, often had special skills which made them useful. For example, warriors from the Middle East were skilled archers, and many other auxiliaries fought in the cavalry. By the 2nd century AD, there were more auxiliaries in the army than legionaries. When they retired, auxiliaries were given Roman citizenship as a reward for their loyalty.

This stone carving shows archers from the Middle East serving as auxiliaries in the Roman army.

WEAPONS OF WAR

The Romans fought most of their battles on open ground, attacking their enemies with javelins and swords. But the Roman army was also highly skilled at besieging and capturing cities. First, the soldiers surrounded the city so that no one could escape and no food or equipment could be brought in. Then, they used catapults to launch rocks at the defenders, and tried to demolish the walls with battering rams.

A SOLDIER'S LIFE

Although the Roman army is famous for its triumphs on the battlefield, there was much more to a soldier's life than just fighting. Many legionaries spent a lot of their time in camps and forts guarding the frontiers of the Empire, or building roads and bridges to help the army move around quickly.

ON THE MOVE

In times of war, legions often had to march for many days to reach a battlefield. The soldiers marched at the same pace for hours, and covered up to 30km (18 miles) a day. When the ground was too boggy or hilly to use carts, they had to carry all their equipment on their backs. If there was no way across a river, they built their own bridge from tree trunks.

Marching soldiers were weighed down with weapons, food, cooking pots and tools for digging.

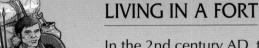

SETTING UP CAMP

When a legion was on the move, the soldiers stopped each night and built a camp. They dug a deep ditch, and used the soil from the ditch to make a rampart - or wall - around the camp. They strengthened the rampart with wooden stakes, and then put up tents in neat rows. The next morning, the soldiers took everything apart and carried it away with them.

LIVING IN A FORT

In the 2nd century AD, the Romans realized they had conquered as much land as they could rule, so most legions were based at permanent frontier forts to protect the borders of the Empire. Life in a Roman fort was strictly organized. Loud trumpet blasts rang around the fort to wake the men in the morning and to announce meal times. Each day, the legionaries were all given a new password, to prevent enemy spies from sneaking into the fort.

Roman forts were organized like small towns, with a bath-house, a shrine and even a law court. Here, you can see part of a typical fort.

There was always a large hospital, since it was vital to keep the soldiers healthy.

In the middle of the fort was the principia, *or headquarters building.*

Granary for storing grain

The bakery was near the edge of the fort, so that fires from the ovens wouldn't destroy the main buildings.

Bath-house

Soldiers fighting mock battles on horseback wore a metal mask and helmet like this.

GOOD AND BAD

Life held many advantages for a Roman soldier - good pay, the chance to keep captured treasure, and better medical treatment than most people received. Retired soldiers were given a large sum of money or a piece of land, and soldiers could also belong to a funeral club, which guaranteed them a proper burial for a small fee.

But there were disadvantages too. During a war, the men lived under the constant threat of injury or death, and in the long stretches of peace, life could become boring, especially since many soldiers served as long as 25 years.

The entire legion had to train every day - an exhausting routine of running, swimming, javelin-throwing and fencing. Soldiers also had to fight mock battles to prepare them for war. Discipline was very strict - if a soldier disobeyed his orders he was beaten, and if a whole legion tried to rebel, one in every ten men was killed.

MASTER BUILDERS

Many soldiers were not only skilled fighters, but also trained builders. In peacetime, they helped to construct canals, bridges and buildings in local towns, and they also built roads throughout the Empire.

How a Roman road was made

Stone slabs formed the road surface.

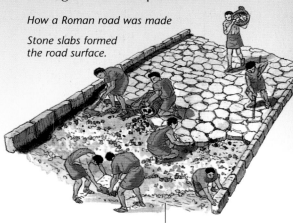

Beneath the surface were layers of sand, gravel and stones packed into a trench.

Roman roads were always as straight as possible, so that a legion could take the most direct route to a troubled area. Even today, many roads in Europe still follow the routes laid down by the Romans.

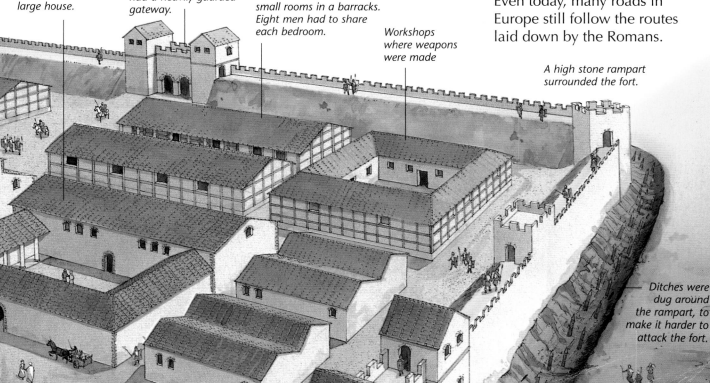

The commanding officer lived in a large house.

Each side of the fort had a heavily guarded gateway.

Most soldiers lived in small rooms in a barracks. Eight men had to share each bedroom.

Workshops where weapons were made

A high stone rampart surrounded the fort.

Ditches were dug around the rampart, to make it harder to attack the fort.

EXPANDING THE EMPIRE

By the end of the Republic in 27BC, the Romans already controlled large areas of Europe, as well as parts of Africa and Asia. Conquering new lands brought Rome wealth and slaves, and emperors were always eager to win glorious victories. Over the next 150 years, Roman territory grew even more, until Rome ruled one of the biggest empires the world has ever seen.

INTO BRITAIN

Britain was first invaded in 55BC by Julius Caesar, but the native tribes refused to accept Roman rule, and Caesar eventually withdrew. In AD43, the Emperor Claudius finally succeeded in conquering the Britons. To celebrate, Claudius held a grand victory parade in Rome and named his son "Britannicus".

TRAJAN'S TRIUMPHS

The Empire reached its greatest extent under the Emperor Trajan, who came to power in AD98. One of the most talented commanders in Roman history, Trajan led his legions on daring campaigns and won huge areas of land. First, he conquered the mountainous land of Dacia (present-day Romania). Then, he led a dangerous mission to the east, creating three new Roman provinces - Armenia, Assyria and Mesopotamia - in just four years.

By AD117, the Empire was at its height. It stretched 4,000km (2,500 miles) from west to east, and was home to more than 50 million people. In Trajan's time, it was possible to travel all the way from the windswept moors of northern Britain to the sunbaked deserts of the Middle East without ever leaving Roman territory.

A statue of the Emperor Trajan

Map of the Roman Empire in AD117, showing all the provinces

BRITANNIA

GERMANIA INFERIOR
GERMANIA SUPERIOR
GALLIA LUGDUNENSIS
BELGICA
RAETIA
AQUITANIA
NORICUM
NARBONENSIS
ALPES POENINAE
PANNONIA
DACIA
MOESIA INFERIOR
TARRACONENSIS
ALPES COTTIAE
ITALIA
DALMATIA
MOESIA SUPERIOR
BITHYNIA AND PONTUS
CAPPADOCIA
LUSITANIA
ALPES MARITIMAE
THRACIA
ARMENIA
BAETICA
CORSICA
MACEDONIA
GALATIA
SARDINIA
EPIRUS
ASIA
MESOPOTAMIA
MAURETANIA CAESARIENSIS
SICILIA
ACHAEA
CILICIA
ASSYRIA
SYRIA
CRETA
LYCIA AND PAMPHYLIA
CYPRUS
MAURETANIA TINGITANA
JUDEA
AFRICA
ARABIA
CYRENAICA
AEGYPTUS

Roman Empire at its largest

REBELLIOUS REGIONS

As the Empire grew larger, it became harder to control, even with the mighty Roman army patrolling its frontiers. As early as AD9, Rome suffered a terrible shock when three whole legions were massacred by tribes deep in the forests of Germany. In AD60, the province of Britain was suddenly plunged into chaos when Boudicca, queen of the native Iceni tribe, led a violent rebellion against the Romans. It took a year to crush the revolt.

A much later artist's view of Queen Boudicca, who poisoned herself after being defeated by the Romans

Another revolt broke out in AD66, in the Middle Eastern province of Judea. Thousands of Jews rebelled, so the Romans destroyed the Jewish capital city, Jerusalem. Then, in AD73, the legions surrounded the mountain-top fortress of Masada, the last stronghold of Jewish resistance. After a siege that lasted an entire year, the Romans stormed the fortress, but found that most of the rebels inside had committed suicide rather than surrender.

HADRIAN'S WALL

In AD117, Hadrian became emperor, and immediately decided that the Empire had grown too vast to control. So he gave up some of the land that Trajan had conquered, and built large permanent fortresses along the new frontiers. To defend Roman Britain against tribes invading from the north, Hadrian built a great wall stretching 130km (80 miles) across the province. Some sections of Hadrian's Wall are still standing today.

INTERNET LINKS
For links to websites where you can watch a short movie about Trajan, take a virtual tour of a fort on Hadrian's Wall, and find out more about Boudicca, go to **www.usborne-quicklinks.com**

Here you can see part of Hadrian's Wall, in northern England.

RUNNING THE EMPIRE

The Roman Empire was so vast, that holding it all together was an enormous task. To make this easier, the Romans organized their territory into lots of different provinces, built a network of roads to link the provinces together, and based lots of soldiers near the Empire's borders to keep out invaders. Latin became the official language of the Empire.

KEEPING THE PEACE

The rule of the Emperor Augustus was the start of a 200-year period with very few major wars inside the Empire. The Romans kept this peace, known as the Pax Romana, with the help of their formidable army. Rebellions were mercilessly crushed. If barbarian tribes began gathering armies outside the Empire, the legions launched an attack to break up the tribes and stop them from uniting against the Romans.

SHOWING RESPECT

Brute force alone wasn't enough to control such a huge area, and the Romans tried to keep people happy by treating them with respect. People in different areas were often allowed to follow their own local customs and worship their own gods.

This stone carving shows a sun god from a temple in England. It combines elements of British and Roman gods.

INTERNET LINKS
For links to websites where you can find an animated map of the expansion of the Roman Empire and learn about Roman roads, go to www.usborne-quicklinks.com

RUNNING THE PROVINCES

Each province was ruled by a governor, who usually came from Rome. Some governors were more important than others. A few vital provinces were ruled by legates, chosen by the emperor himself, while other significant provinces were run by governors appointed by the Senate.

Less important provinces were run by procurators, who were usually wealthy bankers or merchants. There were also many civil servants sent from Rome, who worked alongside the governor and helped to run the provinces.

Early governors weren't paid, and some began to get rich by stealing precious works of art or taking bribes. To stop this from happening, the Emperor Augustus brought in a new system - the governors were paid a salary, and officials were sent from Rome to check up on them.

KEEPING IN TOUCH

Roman roads were used by the army and by traders, but also by imperial messengers, who carried government information on horseback from one part of the Empire to another. All the main roads had post-houses where messengers could stop to get fresh horses. In an emergency, news could travel as far as 240km (150 miles) within a single day.

Imperial messengers were sometimes attacked by rebels from native tribes. Here, you can see a messenger being ambushed by warriors.

A stone carving showing a Roman tax collector at work

COLLECTING TAXES

The Romans collected taxes from all over the Empire, but people in the provinces had to pay much more than those who lived in Italy. At first, the money was collected by tax collectors, but many of these men were corrupt and kept lots of money for themselves. So the Emperor Augustus put the local governors in charge of tax collection.

The taxes helped to pay for the army and for public buildings, such as bath-houses and aqueducts. All this was very expensive and, despite the taxes, the State sometimes ran short of money. The Emperor Marcus Aurelius once had to sell some of his own furniture to raise funds.

CITIZENS OF THE EMPIRE

In 89BC, the Romans allowed anyone living in Italy to become a Roman citizen. Some provincial leaders were also given this privilege, but most people in the provinces were still classed as non-citizens.

The Emperor Caracalla

Then, in AD212, the Emperor Caracalla granted citizenship to every free man living within Roman territory. This gave people a sense of belonging, and helped to unite the different parts of the Empire.

TRAVEL AND TRADE

Travel was vital for the smooth running of the Empire, and every corner of the Roman world was linked to the city of Rome by road, river or sea. Officials came to Rome with reports from distant provinces, important legal cases were brought to the city's courts, and trade goods of every description poured in from all over the Empire and beyond.

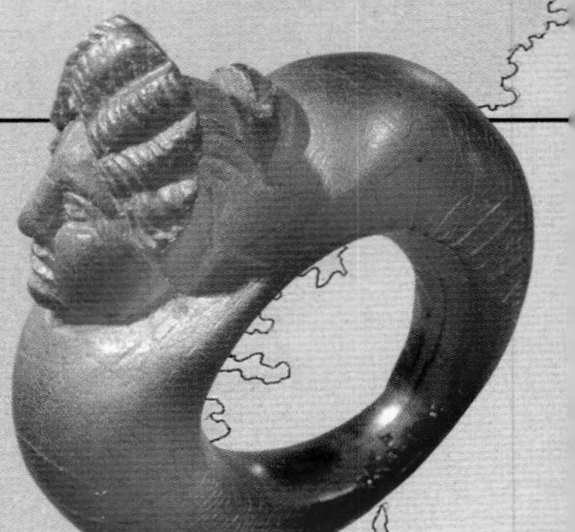

ON THE ROAD

The main purpose of Roman roads was for official business, such as moving troops and supplies or carrying messages to and from the emperor. But the roads were also used by ordinary citizens. Local traders took goods from town to town, while wealthy Romans made frequent trips to the country or the seaside.

Vehicles ranged from light, two-wheeled carriages to heavy, four-wheeled coaches big enough to carry a whole family. If the nearest town was too far away to reach in one day, people could spend the night at a state-run inn. But the rich often preferred to stay with friends, while some Romans took a tent with them or just slept in their carriage.

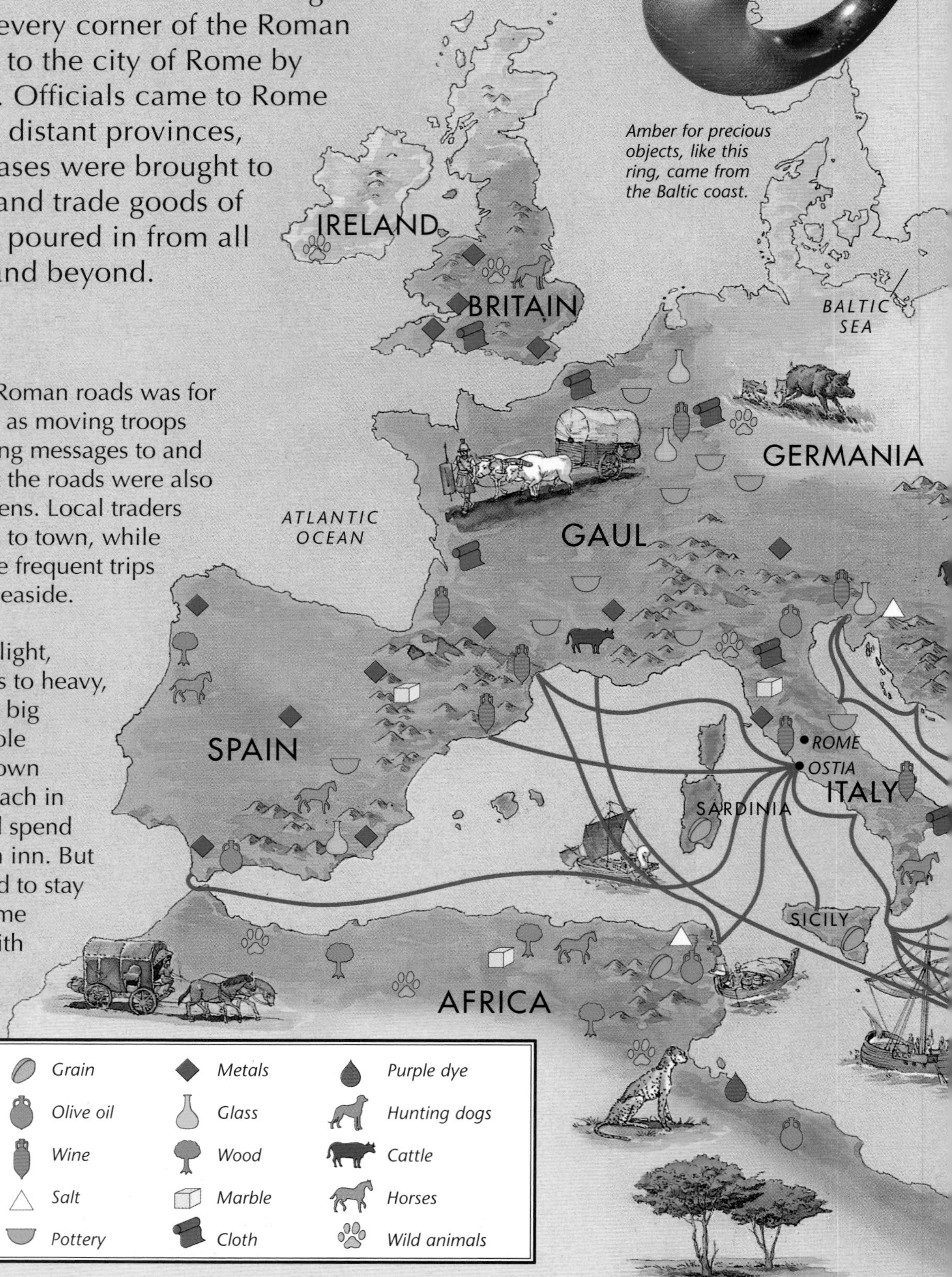

Amber for precious objects, like this ring, came from the Baltic coast.

IRELAND

BRITAIN

BALTIC SEA

GERMANIA

GAUL

ATLANTIC OCEAN

SPAIN

SARDINIA

ROME
OSTIA

ITALY

SICILY

AFRICA

This map shows the goods that came to Rome from different parts of the Empire.

Grain	Metals	Purple dye	
Olive oil	Glass	Hunting dogs	
Wine	Wood	Cattle	
Roman Empire	Salt	Marble	Horses
Trade route	Pottery	Cloth	Wild animals

UNDER SAIL

Despite the excellent roads, it was often easier and cheaper to transport goods by boat. Where possible, the Romans sailed along rivers, but they also had a huge fleet of sea-going merchant ships, which carried goods all over the Mediterranean and as far away as India.

The Mediterranean could be very dangerous to cross, especially in winter. Ships frequently ran into terrible storms, and shipwrecks were common. Roman ships were strong, but they were clumsy and rather slow. With a top speed of only 7km (4 miles) an hour, a ship could take as long as three weeks to sail from Egypt to Italy.

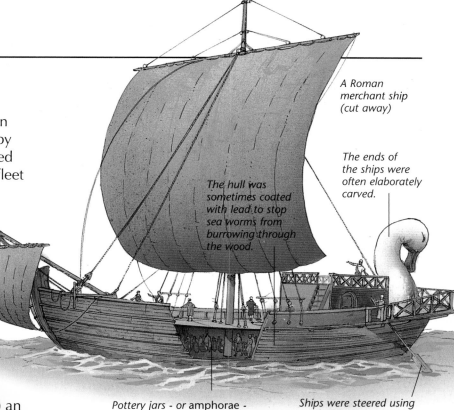

A Roman merchant ship (cut away)

The hull was sometimes coated with lead to stop sea worms from burrowing through the wood.

The ends of the ships were often elaborately carved.

Pottery jars - or amphorae - filled with wine and olive oil

Ships were steered using two oars at the back.

THE PORT OF OSTIA

Most merchant ships were too big to sail up the Tiber to Rome. Instead, they docked at the port of Ostia, at the mouth of the river. There, the cargo was unloaded onto barges and taken the final 25km (15 miles) upriver to Rome. As Rome's main seaport, Ostia was vital to the city's economy and was a busy place packed with merchants, shipbuilders and officials.

WAREHOUSE OF THE WORLD

By the time of the Empire, Rome was at the heart of a vast trading network. Such huge quantities of goods reached the city that one writer described Rome as the "warehouse of the world". While grain, olive oil and wine were the most important items, wealthy Romans could buy an array of luxury goods, such as ivory from East Africa, spices and gems from India and silks from China.

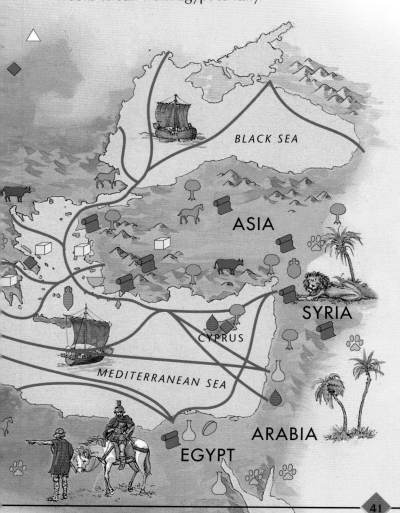

BLACK SEA

ASIA

SYRIA

CYPRUS

MEDITERRANEAN SEA

ARABIA

EGYPT

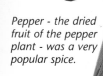

Pepper - the dried fruit of the pepper plant - was a very popular spice.

CRIME AND PUNISHMENT

Everyone in the Empire had to obey Roman laws, and these were usually very strict. People who committed crimes were punished severely, to try to discourage other people from breaking the law. The poor received particularly brutal punishments, which were often carried out in public, but rich citizens were normally treated less harshly.

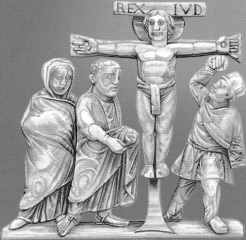

This ivory carving shows Jesus Christ being crucified. The Romans executed many people in this agonizing way.

ON TRIAL

Anyone accused of committing a crime was put on trial in the town basilica. There was a judge in charge of each trial, and a group of citizens - known as the jury - decided whether the accused was innocent or guilty. At important trials, as many as 75 citizens could be asked to serve on the jury.

If the accused could afford it, he paid a lawyer to speak for him. Lawyers often made dramatic and emotional speeches on behalf of their clients. Sometimes, people who were on trial smeared their hair with ashes and wore ragged clothes to make the jury feel sorry for them.

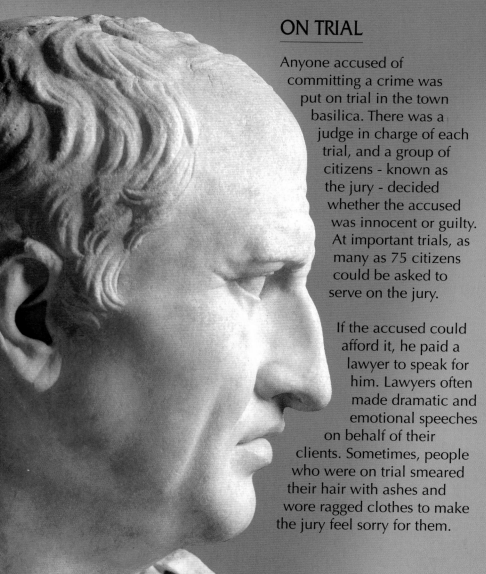

This is a sculpture of Cicero, the most famous of all Roman lawyers. His style of speaking and writing was imitated for centuries after his death.

PAINFUL PUNISHMENTS

When someone was found guilty of a crime, the judge decided what the punishment should be. Wealthy Romans who hadn't paid debts or taxes were often given huge fines. If they couldn't pay up, they lost their property and their citizenship. Other wealthy criminals were exiled to distant parts of the Empire and forbidden to come home.

Many poor people were sold as slaves, forced to work in mines deep underground, or sent out into the arena to fight as gladiators. Some punishments were even worse, and lots of criminals were beheaded, torn apart by wild beasts, or put to death on a cross. (See page 109 for more about the legal system.)

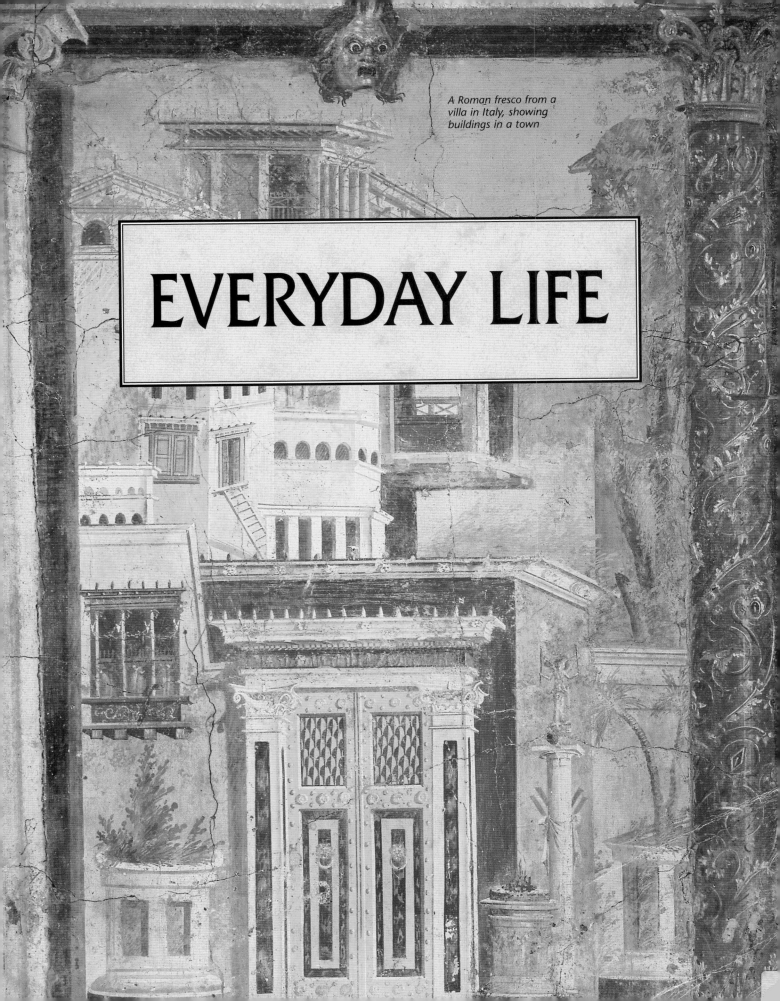

EVERYDAY LIFE

A Roman fresco from a villa in Italy, showing buildings in a town

FAMILY LIFE

The family was an important part of Roman life, and most Romans took their duty to their families very seriously. Families were larger than we are used to today, and normally included the head of the family - known as the *paterfamilias* - his wife and children, his sons' wives and children, and all their slaves.

A FATHER'S POWER

It was a father's duty to look after his family and lead their worship of the household gods (see page 73). During the Republic, the *paterfamilias* was a very powerful figure. He had the right to whip or imprison his children, and could even put them to death or sell them as slaves. But most fathers were affectionate parents, and during the Empire it became a crime for a father to sell or execute his children.

CLIENTS AND PATRONS

As well as the family members who lived with him, a wealthy Roman would also have lots of supporters - or clients - who relied on his help. He was known as their patron. Clients were expected to visit their patron every morning, accompany him whenever he went out, and vote for him if he entered politics. In return, he would help his clients with their career and occasionally ask them to dinner.

WEDDINGS...

Young Romans didn't have much choice about who they married. Their parents usually chose husbands or wives for them - often in order to make an alliance with another powerful or wealthy family. Girls could get married at the age of 12, but their husbands were often much older. When a couple became engaged, a family party was held, and the girl was given a ring for the third finger of her left hand.

An engagement ring engraved with two clasped hands

A 19th-century artist's impression of a couple making offerings on their wedding day

Garlands of myrtle were traditional at Roman weddings.

The night before her wedding, the bride offered her childhood toys to the gods at the household shrine. The next morning, she was dressed in a white tunic, a saffron-yellow cloak and shoes, and a flame-red veil. On her head, she wore a garland of flowers. When the bridegroom and guests arrived, an animal was sacrificed and a priest examined its insides to find out if the gods approved of the marriage.

Then, the marriage contract was read and signed - this gave details of the dowry to be paid by the bride's father to the groom. The bride and groom joined hands and made their vows. After a party at the house of the bride's family, the bride and groom led a procession of flute-players and torch-bearers to the groom's house. The groom carried his bride over the threshold, and the couple began their life together.

...AND FUNERALS

Death was commonplace in Roman families. Many women died in childbirth, and lots of diseases that are curable today were fatal in Roman times. When an important Roman died, the body was washed and covered in oil. If the person was a senator, he was dressed in his official robes. Then, the body lay on display for several days, so visitors could pay their last respects.

On the day of the funeral, the body was carried in a procession to the forum, where a speech was made in praise of the dead person. The body was then either buried or cremated. It was against the law to bury a person's body or ashes inside the city, so Roman tombs were always built outside the city walls.

When a body was cremated, the ashes were placed in an urn like this before being taken to the family tomb.

GROWING UP

Children from all but the poorest homes were brought up to serve the State and improve their family's position in society. Boys were trained for service in the army or the government, while girls were expected to marry well and produce children who would become loyal Roman citizens.

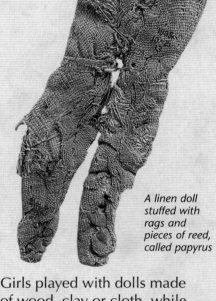

Marbles were made from glass or pottery.

STARTING LIFE

When a child was born, its father would lift it in his arms to show that he accepted it into the family. Every Roman parent wanted a healthy baby boy - baby girls and sickly boys were sometimes left outside to die. Babies were named at eight or nine days old and were given a lucky charm - called a *bulla* - to ward off evil spirits. But many children died in the first few years of life - a woman might have six or seven babies and still end up childless.

A gold bulla like this would have belonged to a child from a very wealthy family.

A linen doll stuffed with rags and pieces of reed, called papyrus

INTERNET LINKS

For links to websites where you can find out about different Roman ball games, and discover what life was like for Roman children,
go to **www.usborne-quicklinks.com**

FUN AND GAMES

Roman children played a wide variety of games, including hide-and-seek, leapfrog and hopscotch. A baby's first toy was usually a pottery rattle, often shaped like a bird, with small pebbles inside. Older children had toy animals, seesaws, swings, hobbyhorses, marbles and hoops for rolling along the ground.

Girls played with dolls made of wood, clay or cloth, while boys had wooden swords. Some lucky children even had miniature chariots pulled by goats or geese.

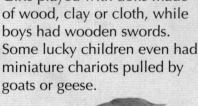

This carving shows a boy riding in a tiny chariot pulled by a goat.

SCHOOL DAYS

Children from poor families had to go out to work at an early age, but families who could afford it sent their children to school when they were seven. Girls and boys were taught together at a school called a *ludus*, where they learned reading, writing and arithmetic. Younger pupils had to recite the alphabet and copy out simple proverbs, while older children read the works of Greek or Roman authors.

A scene in a typical Roman ludus

Most pupils wrote on a wax tablet using a pointed metal pen - called a stylus.

A slave called a *paedagogus* took the children to school and kept an eye on them in class. Most schools only had about 12 pupils, and the school day lasted from dawn until noon without a break. Discipline was very strict, and beatings were common.

Many teachers and tutors were Greeks.

A wooden counting frame - called an abacus

Scroll made of papyrus

Small children scratched writing on pieces of broken pottery.

Pupils left the *ludus* at the age of 11. Boys could continue their education at a secondary school - or *grammaticus* - where they studied Greek and Roman literature, history, geography, astronomy, music, mathematics and athletics. Girls stayed at home and began preparing for marriage. Most Roman men didn't like their women to be too well educated - the poet Juvenal declared: "I hate a woman who reads."

A portrait of a young girl holding a wax tablet and a stylus

BOYS TO MEN

When a boy was about 14, he officially became an adult at a special ceremony held in the forum. He put aside the clothes and *bulla* he had worn as a child and was given an adult's toga. He also had his first shave and was registered as a Roman citizen.

Most young men then began training for the army. Those who wanted to enter politics also had to learn the art of public speaking and were sent to a teacher called a *rhetor*. The richest families sent their sons to Athens or Rhodes to study with the best Greek teachers. This training could continue throughout life - even an experienced politician would take time off work if a good teacher was in town.

ROMAN WOMEN

The ideal Roman woman was a good housekeeper, a caring mother and an obedient wife. She ran the home, took care of her children's early education, and supported her husband in his career. In theory, Roman women had very few rights, but most of them had lots of power behind the scenes.

These mosaic pictures show two Roman women exercising.

WOMEN'S RIGHTS

A Roman husband had the right to divorce his wife if she was childless, if she became ugly or if she argued too much. He could even sentence her to death if she was unfaithful. A wife, on the other hand, could only divorce her husband if he deserted her, joined the army or became a prisoner of war. But although the law was very unfair, Roman history is full of respectful and devoted husbands.

WORKING WOMEN

Not all Roman women could afford to stay at home. Some had jobs as midwives or hairdressers, while many helped out in the family shop or farm. A few women worked as acrobats or dancers, but these jobs weren't considered respectable.

CHANGING TIMES

During Republican times, most women had large families and stayed at home, spinning and weaving cloth. But by the time of the Empire, some wealthy wives had different ideas. Several Roman writers complained about idle women who neglected their duty to have children, and spent their time pampering themselves and attending dinner parties.

POWERFUL WOMEN

Rich women supervised large households with lots of slaves, and a wife often ran her husband's business while he was away. Many politicians' wives took an active interest in their husbands' careers. By crafty plotting and scheming, they made sure that their husbands succeeded in public life, and that their enemies were dealt with mercilessly.

A statue of Livia - wife of Augustus - who was famous for her ruthless scheming. She ended up being declared a goddess.

SLAVES AND FREEDMEN

Most Roman families relied on slaves to help them run their homes, keep their businesses going and farm their land. Slaves were usually bought from dealers or were born into a slave family - they had no rights and belonged entirely to their master or mistress.

HOUSEHOLD SLAVES

Many slaves worked in private homes, doing the shopping, cooking and cleaning. They also served at meals and helped their mistress with her hair, clothes and makeup.

In this painting, you can see a slave arranging a girl's hair.

In many Roman homes, slaves were treated kindly, and sometimes the children of a trusted slave were brought up as companions for their master's children. In the country, slaves worked on farms, and in towns they helped in shops and workshops.

Slaves wore an identity tag inscribed with the name and address of their master.

EDUCATED SLAVES

Many slaves from Greece had a good education and were expensive to buy. They worked in wealthy Roman homes as private tutors, doctors and librarians, or were employed by the government. Well-educated government slaves helped run the Empire, and they often rose to important positions.

A HARD LIFE

For many slaves, life was very hard. Some were made to work in appalling conditions in the mines, while others had to stoke the burning-hot furnaces in the public baths. Many worked on building sites, where they were given all the most dangerous jobs, and some trained as gladiators and had to fight to the death in the arena.

A statuette of a slave cleaning a boot

BECOMING FREE

Slavery wasn't always for life, and some slaves were granted freedom as a reward for loyal service. Other slaves managed to save small amounts of money and buy their own freedom. Very occasionally, a gladiator was freed because he had fought bravely and survived many fights.

Freed slaves were given the status of "freedmen" and could buy property and keep their own slaves. Under some emperors, freedmen could even become Roman citizens. Some of the emperor's freed slaves worked as his personal secretaries and gained great power in the Empire.

LIVING IN A TOWN

The Romans spread their way of life to all the areas they conquered, and built towns all over the Empire. These towns had grand temples, bath-houses and arenas, as well as lots of shops and restaurants. The wealthiest Roman families owned elegant town houses, but most people lived in apartment blocks, called *insulae*.

HOME COMFORTS?

Apartment blocks could be up to seven floors high, and in poor areas of town they were often crowded and dirty. Some of these buildings were so badly built that they collapsed.

This scene shows part of a busy Roman town.

Most apartments had no running water or toilets, so many people used public lavatories. These were very sociable places where people sat side by side and chatted, but you had to pay to use them - poorer people simply used a bucket at home.

Temple

Aqueduct

Public bath-house

Insulae had wooden beams and floors, and they often caught fire.

Insula

Poorer families lived in small rooms at the top.

Toilets were connected to underground drains.

School

Graffiti

Richer people had large, comfortable rooms.

There were shops at street level.

People got water from the fountain.

Bakery

Stepping stones for crossing the street

Butcher's shop

RUNNING WATER

Each town needed fresh water to supply its bath-houses, toilets and drinking fountains. Water was brought down from the hills through a system of pipes and channels, called aqueducts. Waste water was flushed into large sewers under the streets and into a nearby river.

STREET LIFE

Most towns had straight, paved streets laid out in a neat grid pattern. The main streets were broad, but there were narrow alleys too. Often, the streets were full of waste, so stepping stones were built to let people cross without getting filthy.

This photograph shows part of the ruined Roman town of Pompeii.

The streets of a town were lined with dozens of different shops, from butchers and fruit sellers to carpenters and sandal makers. There were also taverns and restaurants, as well as markets where people could buy anything from vegetables to slaves.

MEETING AND GREETING

In the middle of town was a large market square, or forum, where everyone could mingle. There, merchants bought and sold goods, taxes were collected, and people played games. The forum also had a raised platform where town officials stood to make speeches to the crowds.

Around the forum were statues, monuments and temples, and along one side was a huge building called a basilica. The basilica was used as a law court, a town hall and a public meeting place.

There were no drains upstairs, so some people threw their dirty water out of the window, though this was against the law.

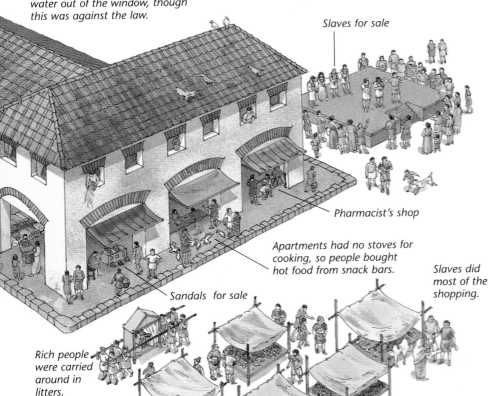

Slaves for sale

Pharmacist's shop

Apartments had no stoves for cooking, so people bought hot food from snack bars.

Sandals for sale

Slaves did most of the shopping.

Rich people were carried around in litters.

INTERNET LINKS
For links to websites where you can take a virtual tour of Pompeii, and see inside a merchant's home, go to www.usborne-quicklinks.com

A HOUSE IN TOWN

Most wealthy Roman families had a comfortable house in town. Although these houses varied in size, each house - or *domus* - followed the same basic design, and was sturdily built from stone, cement and wood. Houses were peaceful, private places, but they were also designed to welcome visitors. Important people made their homes look very grand to impress their guests.

INVITING INTERIORS

Although town houses looked quite plain from the outside, they could be lavishly decorated inside. The walls were often painted with beautiful frescoes, and the floors were laid with stunning mosaics. Lifesize statues in marble or bronze made the rooms look even more dramatic.

FURNITURE

Grand houses were extravagantly furnished with intricately carved marble tables, couches decorated with ivory and gold, and gleaming bronze lamp stands. Sometimes, the floors were covered with leopard skins or fine Egyptian rugs. However, most Roman houses had just a few simple pieces of wooden furniture.

A 19th-century painting showing a Roman family welcoming guests in their atrium

Part of this Roman domus has been cut away, so you can see inside.

"DO COME IN..."

A typical *domus* was arranged around a hall - called the *atrium* - where guests were received. The central part of the ceiling was open to the sky, and beneath the opening was an ornamental pool, known as the *impluvium*. The *atrium* usually had a shrine to the household gods as well.

Around the *atrium* were the dining room, kitchen and study, and the wealthiest homes also had a bathroom. (People who had no bathroom at home used the public bath-house.) The rooms next to the street were often rented out as shops.

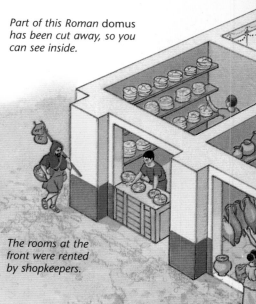

The rooms at the front were rented by shopkeepers.

KEEPING WARM

Wealthy Romans had toilets and running water in their homes, as well as a central heating system, called a *hypocaust*. This ingenious Roman invention was powered by a furnace in the basement, and once the house heated up, it stayed warm for a long time.

IN THE GARDEN

At the back of the house was a peaceful walled garden called a peristyle. The peristyle was often planted with neat hedges, bay trees and rose bushes, and might be decorated with elegant statues, a fountain, or a fish pond. Romans loved to relax and chat in these tranquil, shady places, away from the hustle and bustle of city life.

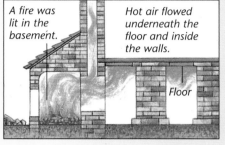

A fire was lit in the basement.

Hot air flowed underneath the floor and inside the walls.

Floor

This diagram shows how a hypocaust worked.

Only the wealthiest families could afford glass windows. Most people covered their windows with animal skins, and wooden shutters kept out the sun, rain and wind.

The garden - or peristyle - was surrounded by a row of columns.

Most houses had two floors, with the bedrooms upstairs.

Tablinum (study)

Lararium (household shrine)

Triclinium (dining room)

Impluvium

Atrium

Kitchen

Storeroom

LIVING IN THE COUNTRY

Although the Roman Empire is famous for its towns, most people actually lived in the country. Many townspeople saw life in the countryside as a peaceful alternative to living in a crowded city. But the reality was anything but relaxing for most country people, and the slaves who worked on farms had to endure hours of backbreaking toil in the fields.

EARLY FARMS

In the early days of the Republic, most farms were small and family-owned. Farmers grew grain, grapes and olives, and kept a few sheep, goats, pigs and cattle. Most farmers produced just enough to feed their families, and any leftover crops were sold in local markets.

This statue shows a Roman farmer using oxen to prepare the land for sowing.

THE RISE OF THE LANDOWNERS

By the 2nd century BC, lots of farmers had to leave Italy to go and fight wars overseas. Many of these men never returned, and their farms fell into ruin. Other farms were devastated by wars in Italy itself.

Rich landowners bought up lots of these ruined farms, combined them to make large estates, and used slaves to work on the estates. Farming became very profitable, and the landowners were some of the wealthiest men in the Roman world.

SLAVES IN THE COUNTRYSIDE

By the time of the Empire, almost all farmworkers were slaves, and they did a variety of exhausting jobs. They had to plant and harvest crops with just a few simple tools, chop down trees to clear new fields, and look after animals.

One of the hardest jobs was being a shepherd. Sheep were often kept in remote highland areas, and the shepherd had to cope with loneliness, bad weather and thieves trying to steal his animals.

A reconstruction of a Roman estate

Fish was a very popular food, and many farms had a pond.

Shepherds often led lonely, isolated lives.

Sheep were kept for wool, milk and meat.

SUPPLYING THE CITIES

Roman cities depended on the countryside for food, building materials, and wood to burn. During the Empire, the most important farm products were grapes and olives - used to make wine and olive oil - and cereals, such as wheat, oats and barley. Farm animals provided townspeople with meat, milk, cheese and wool.

Grapes were a very popular fruit, and were also used to make wine.

Wine was made by trampling grapes to squeeze out the juice, as shown in this stone carving.

Crops such as fruit and vegetables were usually sold to local towns, but olive oil, wine and grain were exported in huge quantities to cities all over the Empire. As Rome grew, farms in Italy could no longer provide enough grain to feed everyone. At the height of the Empire, two-thirds of Rome's grain was imported from Egypt.

Slaves cleared woodland to make new fields.

Farmers grew many different vegetables, such as lettuce, radishes, carrots and beans.

Pigeons were kept to use as food during the winter.

Olive oil was made by crushing olives in a machine like this.

Farmers kept flocks of chickens, ducks and geese for their eggs and meat.

Since the Romans had no sugar, food was sweetened with honey made by bees.

Oxen were used to push machines that harvested wheat.

Pork was a popular meat, so farmers kept large herds of pigs.

A COUNTRY VILLA

Many wealthy Roman families had a large house - or villa - in the countryside, where they went to escape from the stress of city life. The family usually owned all the farmland around their villa, and made lots of money by selling produce from their farm.

EARLY VILLAS

The first villas, built during the Republic, were simple farmhouses surrounded by orchards, vineyards and fields for growing crops and keeping animals. Most of these farms were run by a manager, as the owner usually lived in town.

MAGNIFICENT MANSIONS

As Rome became more prosperous, and more people became wealthy, grand villas were built all over the Empire. The rooms of these villas were often decorated with beautiful mosaics and wall paintings. Some rooms showed scenes of everyday life, while others depicted events from Greek or Roman mythology. The most luxurious houses also had underfloor heating, a bakery, a bath-house and even a swimming pool. The villas near Rome were particularly impressive.

This fresco from the villa of the Empress Livia shows a large Roman villa and part of its garden.

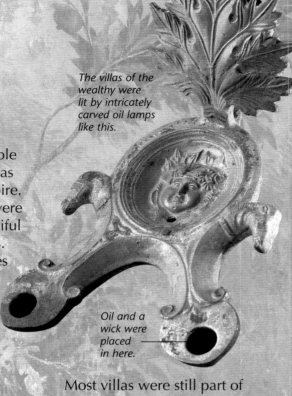

The villas of the wealthy were lit by intricately carved oil lamps like this.

Oil and a wick were placed in here.

Most villas were still part of a farm - or estate - but many were situated well away from the fields. A few of the largest villas had no connection with farming, and were built simply as lavish country homes. The nearby fields only grew food for the owner and his family.

The grandest villas had spacious gardens full of statues and ornamental pools. People relaxed in courtyards surrounded by elegant columns, and the silence was broken only by birdsong and the rippling water of fountains.

INTERNET LINK
For a link to a website where you can take a photo tour of a Roman villa in Germany and find out how the remains of the villa were discovered, go to www.usborne-quicklinks.com

This is an ornamental pool in the gardens of the Emperor Hadrian's villa, near Rome. Known as the Canopus, this part of the villa was inspired by a city in Egypt.

PEACE AND QUIET

Although the Romans were very sociable, they also valued the privacy of their country homes. The Roman writer Pliny remarked that he enjoyed not having to wear a formal toga at his villa. He also appreciated having no one living nearby: "There's peace and quiet all around, which is just as good for your health as the clear sky and pure air."

HADRIAN'S VILLA

One of the most amazing villas was built by the Emperor Hadrian at Tivoli, near Rome. Hadrian designed a group of impressive buildings including a stadium, a library and two bath-houses - all surrounded by splendid gardens. He based some of the buildings on sights he had seen during his travels to Egypt, Greece and other parts of the Empire.

BESIDE THE SEASIDE

Some of the most attractive villas were situated on beautiful stretches of coastline, where their owners could spend summer days bathing in the sea. Fashionable Romans flocked to resorts such as Baiae, on the Bay of Naples, where several emperors built lavish villas. The Emperor Tiberius had no fewer than 12 villas on the island of Capri, just off the Italian coast.

FOOD AND COOKING

Some foods which we take for granted today, such as potatoes, tomatoes and chocolate, were unknown to the Romans. Likewise, many Roman dishes are unheard of now. The menu at a lavish banquet could include sows' udders and larks' tongues, though most people never ate such extravagant meals.

Glass bottles like these were used to store oils and sauces.

THREE MEALS A DAY?

Poorer Romans and slaves had to live on basic food, such as bread, porridge and stew, but wealthier people had a more varied diet. For breakfast, they ate a snack of bread or wheat biscuits with honey, and lunch was a simple meal of eggs, cheese, cold meat and fruit.

Many people hardly ate at all during the day, waiting instead for the evening meal. For average Romans, this was roast poultry or fish, but the wealthy often enjoyed lavish dinner parties.

INTERNET LINKS
For a link to a website where you'll find a selection of tasty Roman recipes, and instructions for cooking them go to
www.usborne-quicklinks.com

WINE AND WATER

The Romans drank lots of wine, and people in Rome could choose from around 200 types which were made all over the Empire. Wine was often spiced, or sweetened with honey, and was usually diluted with water - drinking it undiluted wasn't considered respectable.

In the early days of the Republic, women were forbidden to drink wine, but during the Empire this rule was dropped. Other popular drinks included grape juice and goat's milk, and people could also drink water from public fountains.

IN THE KITCHEN

A Roman kitchen was equipped with many of the same utensils that we use today - saucepans, cheese graters, and strainers to drain water away. These items were usually made of bronze, which can make food taste strange, so some pans were coated with silver.

Food was boiled, fried, grilled, stewed, or roasted on a spit. With no freezers or cans to keep food fresh, it had to be smoked, pickled or salted to preserve it.

This scene shows slaves preparing a meal in a Roman kitchen.

Wine and oil were stored in tall earthenware pots called amphorae.

SPICES AND SAUCES

Rich Romans loved spicy food, and most of their meals were highly seasoned or eaten with a strong sauce. One of the most popular sauces was a thick, salty concoction called *liquamen*, also known as *garum*, made from pickled fish.

Because there was no chimney, smoke often billowed around the kitchen.

Most dishes were seasoned with herbs.

Food was cooked in earthenware or bronze pots.

Meat was roasted on a spit.

Charcoal was burned in the stove.

Slaves often spent all day preparing the evening meal.

Ingredients for sauces were ground up with a pestle and mortar.

EATING OUT

In towns, very few people did their own cooking. Most people lived in apartment blocks with wooden beams and floors, and it was forbidden to light cooking fires inside, in case the building burned down. Instead of cooking at home, people usually bought hot food, such as pies, sausages and stews, from snack bars in the street.

AT A DINNER PARTY

Wealthy Romans loved to eat fancy food and they often threw lavish dinner parties. Hosting a party was a great way for people to show off their wealth and power, and important Romans tried to outdo each other by making their banquets more and more extravagant.

THE PARTY BEGINS

A dinner party usually began in the early evening. The guests would remove their sandals at the door and have their feet washed by a slave, before being announced by an usher. They would then be shown to their places and have their hands washed with perfumed water. Having clean hands was important since people usually ate with their fingers.

Wealthy Romans reclined on cushioned couches while they ate - only slaves and children sat on chairs to eat. Men and women ate together, with up to nine people around the table.

The host of the party sat here.

Romans didn't have forks, but they sometimes used knives and spoons.

People ate straight from a serving dish, rather than using plates.

Between courses, slaves washed the guests' hands with perfumed water.

This scene shows wealthy Romans at a dinner party.

The guests reclined on three couches.

Musicians entertained the guests.

FUN AND GAMES

Between courses, the guests were entertained by poets, musicians, conjurors or clowns, and after dinner there would often be games. For example, the host would pick a number, and everyone would have to swallow that number of drinks.

TABLE MANNERS

To show that they had enjoyed a meal, guests would belch loudly, and if they were too full to finish their food, they could wrap the leftovers in a napkin to take home. Really greedy guests would simply tickle their throats with a feather until they were sick, and then start eating all over again. The writer Seneca was disgusted by guests who indulged in this habit, and wrote scornfully: "They vomit to eat, and eat to vomit."

Beautifully decorated drinking cups like this were used at grand parties.

FRIGHTENING FEASTS

Guests had to be careful what they talked about at parties, as the emperor's spies were everywhere. If people were overheard criticizing the emperor, they might suddenly be tied up in chains and dragged away. Some parties were even more dangerous - the crazy emperor Elagabalus once smothered his guests to death with thousands of rose petals falling from the ceiling.

A 19th-century painting of Elagabalus's guests being smothered in petals. The petals were released from a net above the table.

MARATHON MEALS

A full Roman banquet was made up of seven courses, and could last as long as ten hours. It started with a few cold courses, such as eggs, sardines and mushrooms, before moving on to more exciting dishes, like dormice in honey, flamingoes' tongues or even elephants' trunks.

The way the food looked was just as important as how it tasted, and chefs particularly enjoyed disguising one type of food as another. The writer Petronius boasted that his chef could make a pig's belly look just like a fish.

FASHION AND BEAUTY

Looking good was very important to the Romans, and wealthy men and women spent a lot of time on their appearance. Fashions were often influenced by what the emperor and his wife wore, and people tried hard to keep up with the latest trends.

TUNICS AND TOGAS

The main garment for men was a tunic, made out of two rectangles of wool stitched together and tied with a belt. Underneath, men wore a loincloth - an ancient version of underpants made from a strip of wool or linen.

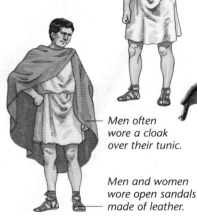

Most men wore short, undyed tunics like this.

Men often wore a cloak over their tunic.

Men and women wore open sandals made of leather.

Over their tunic, Roman citizens sometimes wore a toga - a large piece of woollen cloth wrapped carefully around the body. But the toga was so uncomfortable that it was usually only worn on important public occasions.

A statue of the Emperor Augustus wearing a toga

STOLAS AND PALLAS

Underwear for women consisted of a loincloth and sometimes a simple leather bra. On top of these went a long robe called a stola and a large rectangular shawl, known as a palla.

Women often wore their palla draped around their shoulders.

A woman in a bright silk stola

The palla could also be looped over the head like a hood.

During the Empire, fashionable Roman ladies began to wear brightly dyed stolas and pallas, made from Indian cotton or Chinese silk. These materials were incredibly expensive, and silk was literally worth its weight in gold.

STATUS SYMBOLS

Clothes were an important way of showing a person's status, and people had to adhere to strict rules. Only Roman citizens were allowed to dress in a toga. Purple was the most expensive dye, and only the wealthiest people could afford it. Two broad purple stripes at the front marked a senator's tunic, while two narrow stripes signified the *equites*. Consuls wore a purple band along one of the long sides of their togas. It was a crime for anyone except the emperor to dress entirely in purple.

HAIR CARE

For most of the Roman era, men were clean-shaven and had simple, short haircuts - although the Emperor Hadrian later started a fashion for beards. Most men went to the barber every morning for a shave. This was a good opportunity to hear the latest gossip, but it was also very painful because barbers didn't use any soap or oil. Some men removed the hair from their arms and legs too.

During the Republic, women usually tied their hair in a simple bun, but in later times many had extremely elaborate hairstyles. Their hair would be curled with heated tongs, then arranged in an intricate pile held in place by dozens of hairpins. Some women cut off a slave's hair and had it made into a wig.

This statue shows a popular women's hairstyle from the 2nd century AD. The poet Juvenal mocked hairstyles like this, saying they made women look much taller from the front than the back.

RINGS ON THEIR FINGERS

Rich Roman men and women wore lots of rings, sometimes several on each finger. Wealthy women also wore a glittering variety of gold and silver brooches, bracelets, necklaces and earrings.

A gold ring set with a carved gemstone

A necklace set with emeralds and mother-of-pearl

A pair of intricately carved earrings, shaped like dolphins

A bracelet shaped like a snake

AMAZING MAKEUP

A wealthy Roman woman would spend hours every morning being made up by her slaves. It was fashionable to look pale, so women whitened their faces and arms with powdered chalk. They used ash to darken their eyebrows, and painted their lips red with plant dye. Some even used a face cream made from crushed snails.

Wealthy women wore perfume, which they kept in beautiful bottles like this.

AT THE BATHS

Very few Roman houses had a bathroom, so most people made a daily trip to the public bath-house. But a visit to the baths involved much more than just a good wash. The largest bath-houses were vast leisure complexes where people could exercise, meet friends, discuss business and politics, or simply relax.

POOLS OR PALACES?

By AD300, the city of Rome had 11 public baths - or *thermae* - and about 1,000 privately owned bath-houses where people could bathe in greater privacy. Some emperors built spectacular public baths, gleaming with gold and marble, to show off their wealth and power. The most impressive baths were those built by the Emperor Caracalla, which could hold up to 1,600 people at a time.

PAYING YOUR WAY

Entrance to the baths was extremely cheap, especially for men, who were only charged a *quadrans* - the smallest Roman coin. Women had to pay four times that amount, but children got in free. Wealthy politicians sometimes tried to win votes by paying everyone's fees for a day.

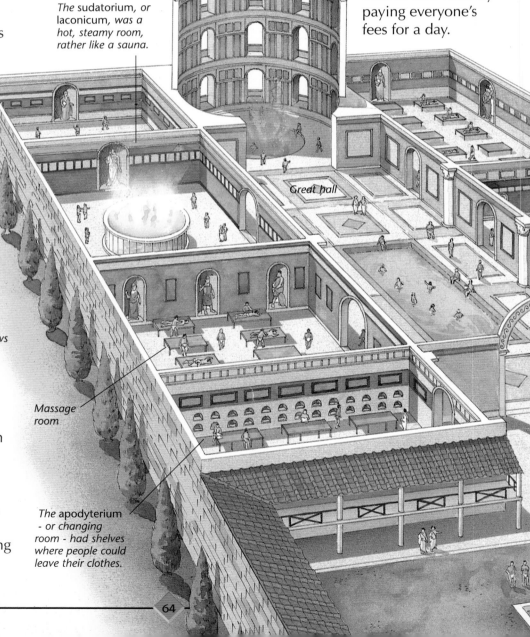

The *caldarium, another very hot room,* had a hot pool. This was where people got themselves clean.

The *sudatorium, or* laconicum, *was a hot, steamy room, rather like a sauna.*

Great hall

This reconstruction shows the different rooms in a Roman bath-house.

Massage room

The *apodyterium - or changing room - had shelves where people could leave their clothes.*

BATH TIME

The baths were usually open from mid-morning until sunset, and most Romans went every day - women in the morning and men in the afternoon. For most of the Roman period, mixed bathing was considered scandalous.

WORKING OUT

Many Romans began their visit to the baths by working up a sweat in the exercise yard - or *palaestra*. Men enjoyed weight-lifting, wrestling, fencing and ball games, while women played a game called *trochus*, which involved rolling a metal hoop with a hooked stick.

GETTING CLEAN

The Romans didn't have soap, so instead they smeared their bodies with perfumed oil. The oil was then scraped off, along with the dirt, using a curved stick called a *strigil*. Scraping yourself wasn't easy, so wealthy Romans usually brought a slave to do the scraping for them.

This is a metal strigil - *the long, curved end was scraped over the skin.*

THE HOTTEST SPOT IN TOWN

The baths were heated by a central heating system, or *hypocaust*. Hot air, warmed by a furnace in the basement, ran under the floors and inside the walls. Some of the floors were so hot that people had to wear wooden-soled sandals to stop their feet from getting burned, while the slaves who stoked the furnaces often fainted from the heat.

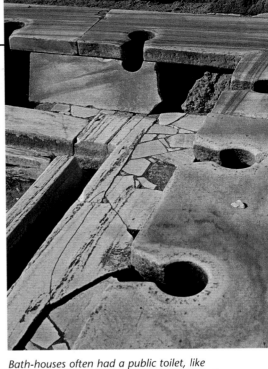

Bath-houses often had a public toilet, like this, where people sat together and chatted.

"...AND RELAX!"

Roman men often stayed at the baths until closing time. After their bath, they could buy a snack at one of the food stalls, then stroll in the gardens, read quietly in the library, or listen to a concert or poetry recital. Some sat in the shade playing board games, such as chess or backgammon, or gambling with dice.

A selection of games counters and dice

The tepidarium *had a lukewarm - or tepid - pool, where bathers could gradually cool down.*

The bath ended with a refreshing dip in the frigidarium - *an unheated, open-air swimming pool.*

AT THE GAMES

Most Roman citizens had a lot more free time than people do today, because most of the heavy work was done by slaves. In fact, there were so many slaves in Rome that many poorer Romans couldn't find jobs at all. To keep people entertained - and leave them less time for stirring up trouble - the emperor put on bloodthirsty shows known as "the Games", where people could watch gladiator fights and wild-beast hunts.

On sunny days, a huge awning was hung from poles around the top of the Colosseum.

Women weren't allowed to sit with men. They had to watch from behind this wall.

The seating has been cut away so you can see inside.

The floor of the arena was sometimes flooded so that gladiators could take part in mock sea battles.

THE GROWTH OF THE GAMES

Gladiator fights were originally held as part of ancient funeral ceremonies. But during the Republic, politicians realized they could win votes by putting on lavish shows, and the number of days given to the games grew. By imperial times, there were 93 days of games in the year, and more were added by emperors eager to make themselves popular.

The Games were first held in a wooden stadium erected especially for the events. By AD81, a huge stone stadium with an oval arena in the middle had been built in Rome to hold the Games. Known as the Flavian Amphitheatre, or later, the Colosseum, it was the largest stadium in the Empire, and could hold up to 50,000 people at a time.

A BEASTLY PASTIME

A day at the arena began with a grand parade of gladiators, musicians, dancers, jugglers and priests. Then, the wild beasts were brought out. Rare animals were put on display or were made to perform circus tricks. According to the Roman historian Suetonius, one emperor introduced the amazing spectacle of tightrope-walking elephants.

Most animals were forced to fight each other or were hunted down with spears, daggers, bows and arrows. Sometimes, unarmed criminals were dragged into the arena to be torn to pieces by lions, tigers or bears.

In beast hunts, like the one shown here, as many as 5,000 animals might die in a single day.

GLADIATORS

Gladiator fights took place in the afternoon. Most gladiators were slaves, criminals or prisoners of war who were forced to fight each other, but some were paid volunteers. A very small number of gladiators were women. There were many types of gladiators, each with different weapons and costumes, and different types were usually pitted against each other.

Gladiators often fought to the death, although anyone who was badly wounded could appeal to the emperor for mercy. After consulting the crowd, the emperor gave a signal with his thumb. Experts think the "thumbs up" sign meant that the gladiator should be allowed to live.

Victorious gladiators received money and a crown, and those who survived long enough could become rich and famous - a little like today's rock stars. After many victories, a gladiator might be given a wooden sword, which meant that he was a free man. Many freed fighters became trainers at special gladiator schools.

The retiarius *fought with a net and trident.*

The murmillo *was a heavily armed gladiator who wore a helmet crowned with a fish.*

The Samnite carried a sword and shield, and wore a helmet with a visor.

The Thracian had a curved dagger and a small, round shield.

INTERNET LINKS
For links to websites where you can prepare a gladiator for battle, see their weapons and tour the Colosseum, go to **www.usborne-quicklinks.com**

AT THE RACES

Chariot races were originally part of religious festivals, but soon became incredibly popular as entertainment. Races were held at specially designed racetracks, called circuses, and regularly attracted huge crowds. The largest racetrack was the *Circus Maximus* in Rome, which could seat 250,000 people - more than any sports stadium in the world today.

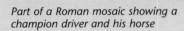

Part of a Roman mosaic showing a champion driver and his horse

THE DAY BEGINS

Only Roman citizens and their families could go to the races, and people started arriving at dawn to get a good seat. Unlike at the Games, men and women could sit together. The poet Ovid wrote that the circus was a good place to find a girlfriend or boyfriend!

The spectacle began with a parade, as musicians led in the official who was to start the races. This might be an important senator, or even the emperor himself. He and his attendants were followed by singers, and priests carrying images of the gods.

Chariots raced around the central barrier - or spina - which had three pillars at each end.

The poorest citizens stood at the back.

Marble seats for senators

Imperial box

Internet links For links to websites where you can find out more about chariot races in ancient Rome, go to **www.usborne-quicklinks.com**

"...AND THEY'RE OFF!"

At the blast of a trumpet, the official in charge raised a white cloth and let it fall to the ground. The starting gates at one end of the track flew open, and the drivers charged out on their lightweight chariots, racing counter-clockwise around the track.

The chariots were normally pulled by two or four horses, but for added excitement six or eight horses might be used. The more horses there were, the harder the chariot was to control. To stop themselves from falling off, drivers wound the reins around their bodies. Each driver wore a light helmet and carried a dagger, so he could cut himself free if his chariot overturned.

Here you can see chariots rounding the corner in a race at the Circus Maximus.

TAKING THE CORNER

The most hair-raising part of the race came as the drivers turned the tight corner at each end of the track. Jostling for position, they tried to stay as close as possible to the central barrier - or *spina*. Chariots often collided, resulting in spectacular crashes, and it was common for drivers to be injured or killed.

FAME AND FORTUNE

Most drivers were slaves, but some were professionals who were paid large amounts of money to compete. Race winners were rewarded with more money, a palm leaf of victory and instant fame. The life of a chariot-driver was glamorous, but could be short - many drivers died in their early 20s.

TEAM SPIRIT

Most chariot-drivers belonged to one of four teams - red, blue, white or green - and the best drivers were idolized by their team's supporters. Fans placed bets on their team before a race, and cheered their drivers on noisily. Passions ran so high that serious riots sometimes broke out between rival groups of fans.

The palm leaf was the Roman symbol of victory.

At the end of each of the seven laps, a marker in the shape of an egg or a dolphin was turned over.

Up to 12 chariots competed in each race, with as many as 24 races in a day.

This Egyptian monument, called an obelisk, was brought to Rome by the Emperor Augustus.

The track measured 550m x 180m (1,800ft x 600ft).

69

PLAYS AND PANTOMIMES

The idea of drama came from Ancient Greece, and plays based on Greek tragedies and comedies became popular in Rome during the 3rd century BC. But the Romans gradually developed their own style of drama - one that could compete with the thrills and spills of chariot races and gladiator shows.

TRAGEDY AND COMEDY

The first plays seen in Rome were translations of Classical Greek plays - both tragedies and comedies. Tragedies were about Greek gods and heroes, while comedies dealt with ordinary people. Roman writers soon began adapting these plays to make them more interesting for a Roman audience. The most famous playwrights are Plautus and Terence, whose comedies were popular during the 2nd century BC.

DRAMATIC CHANGES

At first, plays were staged in temporary wooden buildings, as part of a festival for a god or goddess, and the whole building was taken down as soon as the festival was over. The first permanent auditorium in Rome - the *Theatrum Pompeii* - was built in 55BC, and similar buildings were soon put up in towns all over the Empire.

Plays were accompanied by music performed on instruments such as the lyre.

Classical plays, with their complicated plots and dialogue, remained popular among some educated Romans, but most people wanted something much less demanding. So speeches were cut and plays were reduced to a series of songs sung by a chorus, with actors miming the action. This type of drama was called pantomime.

MASKS AND COSTUMES

Each play featured the same kind of characters, such as the "wise old man" or the "smiling fool", and the actors wore striking masks to show which character they were playing. Female characters wore pale masks, but behind the masks all the actors were men.

Different characters could also be identified by the actors' robes - red for a poor person, purple for a rich citizen and white for an elderly character.

In this mosaic, a group of actors is getting ready to perform a play. The man on the left is being helped into his costume.

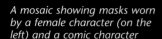
A mosaic showing masks worn by a female character (on the left) and a comic character

TROUBLE AHEAD

During the Empire, a style of drama known as mime became very popular. Mime actors wore normal clothes, without masks, and women were allowed to take part. Plays were either very rude or very violent, and the action was as realistic as possible.

At the end of one particular play, a criminal took the place of an actor and was actually tortured to death on stage.

STARS OF THE SHOW

The Romans didn't think acting was a respectable profession, so actors were usually slaves or freedmen. But famous actors were treated like heroes, and some became so popular that they were mobbed by their fans. Women weren't allowed to sit near the stage, in case they were tempted to run off with one of the performers.

These are the ruins of a Roman auditorium in Merida, in western Spain. The stage building is in the middle, with the tiered stone seating on the right.

INTERNET LINK
For a link to a website with a reconstruction of a Roman auditorium and more information about Roman plays, go to **www.usborne-quicklinks.com**

GODS AND GODDESSES

The Romans had two kinds of gods - the powerful gods and goddesses of the state religion and the friendly household spirits who protected their homes. Temples were built for important state gods, and people were expected to attend public sacrifices. At home, the Romans prayed to their own household spirits and offered them simple gifts.

MANY GODS

There were dozens of Roman gods and goddesses, but the three most important ones were Jupiter, Juno and Minerva. Most Roman gods were borrowed from the Greeks - Jupiter was originally the Greek god Zeus.

Each god controlled a different aspect of life. Jupiter ruled the sky, Juno was the goddess of women, and Minerva looked after soldiers and school children. There were even household spirits responsible for mildew. You can see a list of Roman gods on page 102.

The Romans believed that thunderstorms were caused by their chief god, Jupiter, hurling thunderbolts from the sky.

MAKING SACRIFICES

Offerings to the gods ranged from simple cakes and flowers to elaborate statues, but the most popular gifts were animals. Sacrificing a valuable animal was meant to show the gods how much people cared about them. Priests sacrificed oxen, sheep, pigs and doves on open-air altars in front of temples.

Once the creature had been killed, its internal organs were taken out and examined. The Romans believed that this would help them find out the will of the gods. Then, the organs were burned on the altar, and the rest of the meat was served up as a feast for the god's followers.

Bacchus was the god of wine. This statue shows him with bunches of grapes entwined in his hair.

PRIESTS AND PRIESTESSES

Most Roman priests had other jobs too, and by the time of the Empire, the chief priest - or *Pontifex Maximus* - was the emperor himself. But one group of priestesses - the Vestal Virgins - devoted most of their lives to their goddess. Vesta was goddess of the hearth, and the Vestal Virgins kept a constant fire burning in her temple in Rome.

A priest leading a bull to be sacrificed outside a temple

One of the leading Roman priests was the *Flamen Dialis*, or Priest of Jupiter. His life was made very complicated by a huge number of rules. For example, he couldn't touch or even talk about goats, ivy or beans.

INTERNET LINKS
For links to websites where you can find out about lots of Roman gods and goddesses, and test your knowledge with online quizzes, go to **www.usborne-quicklinks.com**

FESTIVALS

Religious festivals took place throughout the year, but especially at sowing and harvest times. Some festivals were very solemn occasions, but others were great fun. During the mid-winter feast of *Saturnalia*, masters waited on their slaves, people exchanged gifts, and a mock-king ruled over the merrymakers.

EMPEROR GODS

Very soon after the Emperor Augustus died, he was declared a god by the next emperor, Tiberius. After this, many emperors became gods when they died, and statues were put up all over the Empire so people could worship their past rulers.

Praying to dead emperors was really just a way of showing respect for Rome, but the Emperor Caligula actually believed he was a god. According to the Roman historian Suetonius, Caligula often dressed up as Jupiter and even carried a metal thunderbolt to make himself seem more frightening.

GODS AT HOME

In their own homes, the Romans prayed to two main groups of gods. The *lares* were spirits who protected the home, while the *penates* looked after the larder and the food cupboards.

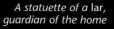

A statuette of a lar, *guardian of the home*

Each house had a shrine - called the *lararium* - where the family held daily prayers and offered food and wine to their gods. On special occasions, such as birthdays and weddings, the spirits were given extra gifts.

The lararium *shown here was found in a house at Pompeii. The family would have placed their gifts in front of the statuettes*

BELIEFS AND SUPERSTITIONS

By the time of the Empire, most Romans felt that the worship of the state gods had become formal and empty, but this didn't mean that religion was dead. People still believed that gods and spirits could affect their lives, and the Romans saw signs - or omens - everywhere.

A bronze sculpture of a hand covered with symbols to ward off evil spirits

SIGNS AND SUPERSTITIONS

The Romans were incredibly superstitious. They believed that some days were unlucky, and that owls, snakes and black cats were messengers of disaster. Even educated Romans were terrified of ghosts. People wore lucky charms to ward off evil spirits, and performed complex rituals to bring themselves good fortune.

TELLING THE FUTURE

People tried many ways of looking into the future. Priests called augurs interpreted the patterns made by birds, clouds and stars. Army generals tried to predict success in battle by watching the way sacred chickens ate their food, and anxious emperors questioned astrologers to learn if they would be assassinated.

At times of national crisis, the Romans consulted the writings of the Sibyl of Cumae. She was a wise woman who lived in a cave at the time of the Roman kings and claimed to be able to see into the future.

FOREIGN FAITHS

By the 1st century AD, many people were looking for a faith that would give their lives more meaning, and thousands of Romans turned to the religions of the Middle East. Unlike the state religion, these foreign faiths had strict rules on how their followers should live. They also offered believers the promise of a happy life after death.

MOTHER GODDESSES

Romans throughout the Empire became passionate followers of Isis, from Egypt, and Cybele, from Turkey. These powerful mother goddesses attracted mainly female followers, and their priests held elaborate rituals on the themes of death and rebirth. Worship of Isis became especially popular after the Egyptian queen Cleopatra spent a year in Rome in 45BC.

Priests of Isis shook a rattle, called a sistrum.

This picture shows a ceremony outside a temple of the Egyptian goddess Isis.

Temples were decorated with Egyptian-style statues.

The chief priest chanted prayers to Isis.

Sacred birds called ibises were kept at the temple.

Priests played musical instruments and sang songs.

MIGHTY MITHRAS

Followers of the Persian god Mithras met in underground temples and suffered terrifying ordeals, such as being locked in a coffin for several hours. Only men could worship Mithras, and his religion was especially popular with the Roman army.

Here, Mithras is shown slaying a sacred bull, whose blood was believed to have given birth to the Earth.

JEWS AND CHRISTIANS

The Middle Eastern religions of Judaism and Christianity each had a single god, which meant that their followers couldn't worship the Roman gods as well. This led to fierce campaigns against Christians and Jews in the Empire. Thousands of Christians were persecuted and put to death, and the Emperor Hadrian tried to get rid of Judaism completely.

CELTIC GODS

In the Celtic countries of Britain and Gaul (present-day France), the Romans prayed to many native gods, and sometimes combined these gods with their own Roman deities. But the Romans loathed the Celtic priests - called druids - because they performed human sacrifices, and also because they encouraged the Celts to resist Roman rule.

INTERNET LINKS

For links to websites where you can take a virtual tour of a temple of Mithras and watch a slide show about Roman religious beliefs, go to www.usborne-quicklinks.com

HEALING THE SICK

In Roman times, no one knew exactly what caused diseases, so if people became sick they blamed evil spirits, or thought that the gods were punishing them. The Romans tried many ways to cure themselves, including asking their gods for help.

SPELLS AND PRAYERS

Many Romans tried to drive away diseases by chanting magic spells, or by praying to Aesculapius, the god of healing.

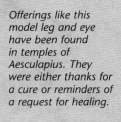

Offerings like this model leg and eye have been found in temples of Aesculapius. They were either thanks for a cure or reminders of a request for healing.

Some people were so desperate for a cure that they spent all night in the temple of Aesculapius in Rome. They hoped that the god would visit them in a dream, and show them how to make themselves well.

HERBAL MEDICINES

This carving shows a pharmacist's shop. Unusually for Roman times, the pharmacist is a woman.

Most Roman medicines were made from herbs and plants. In the early days of the Republic, people brewed their own medicines, using traditional recipes, but by the time of the Empire pharmacists had set up shops selling herbal remedies.

Pharmacists ground up plants and minerals with a pestle and mortar and made them into pills or sticks of ointment. They also made an alcoholic cough mixture by combining wine and herbs.

Rosemary was used in remedies for bad eyesight.

INTERNET LINKS
For links to websites where you can read about Roman doctors, medicine and remedies, and try to solve a mysterious death, go to **www.usborne-quicklinks.com**

VISITING THE DOCTOR

Wealthy Romans paid for a doctor to come to their house, but most people had to visit the doctor themselves. Medical treatment wasn't free, but in AD100 a state health service was set up, so the poor could see a doctor free of charge.

Surgeries were held in shops or private rooms, and patients lay on a couch while a doctor examined them. Doctors prescribed herbal medicines, advised on a healthy diet, and recommended exercise and visits to the baths. However, they also believed in the helpful effects of blood-letting, and drained away cupfuls of their patients' blood.

Sage was an important ingredient in cough mixture

EYES AND TEETH

Some doctors specialized in treating eyes. They made sticks of eye ointment from lead, zinc or iron and even performed operations to remove cataracts. Dentists extracted rotten teeth, and supplied false ones to fill in the gaps.

False teeth made from ivory or bone were attached to a gold band which wouldn't rust.

SCARY SURGERY

Surgeons who had trained in the army performed basic operations in state hospitals. These doctors were expert at sawing off limbs and setting bones, but they were less successful at what we would see as simple operations, such as removing an appendix.

This bronze spoon was used for giving liquid medicines.

Surgeons removed spearheads from wounds with forceps like these.

Doctors used this instrument to help them carry out internal examinations.

This is a spatula, which was used for applying ointment.

This surgical hook was useful for holding wounds open during operations.

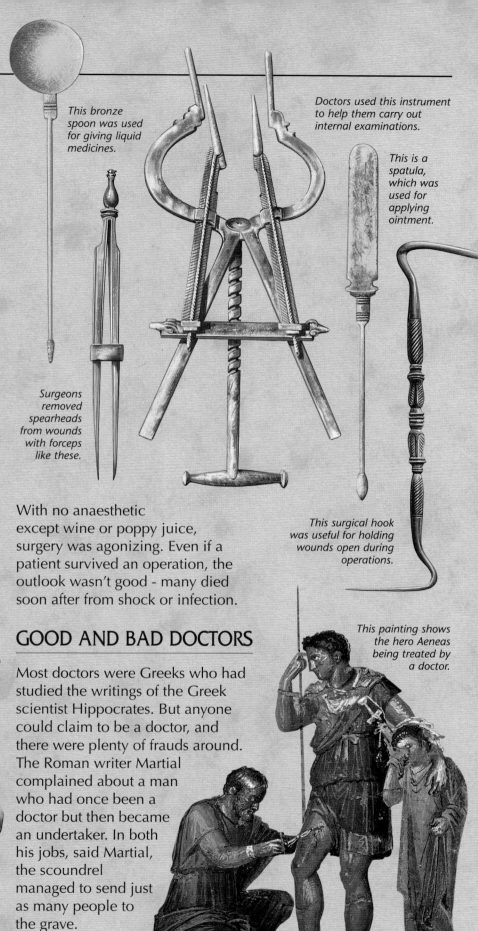

With no anaesthetic except wine or poppy juice, surgery was agonizing. Even if a patient survived an operation, the outlook wasn't good - many died soon after from shock or infection.

GOOD AND BAD DOCTORS

Most doctors were Greeks who had studied the writings of the Greek scientist Hippocrates. But anyone could claim to be a doctor, and there were plenty of frauds around. The Roman writer Martial complained about a man who had once been a doctor but then became an undertaker. In both his jobs, said Martial, the scoundrel managed to send just as many people to the grave.

Mustard seeds were used to treat snakebites.

Fennel was supposed to calm the nerves.

Lemon balm was believed to cure headaches.

Garlic was given to soldiers to keep them healthy.

This painting shows the hero Aeneas being treated by a doctor.

CRAFTS AND TRADES

All the heavy work in a Roman town was done by slaves, so ordinary citizens had to earn their living in other ways. Most townspeople worked as shopkeepers or craftworkers, and Roman towns and cities were filled with bustling shops and workshops.

A carving of a knife-maker and his wife at the counter of their workshop

SHOPKEEPERS

Each town had several bakers, butchers, fishmongers, olive oil sellers and wine merchants, who supplied people's daily needs. The baker was especially important because everyone needed bread.

In this picture of a busy baker's shop, the roof has been cut away so you can see inside.

CRAFTWORKERS

Roman craftworkers produced a huge variety of goods, ranging from basic clothes and tools to fancy goblets and statues. Usually, the craftworkers were men, but Roman wives and daughters also helped in the family workshop. Sons learned their trade by working with their fathers, but slaves were kept to do the nastiest jobs.

The same essential craftworkers were found in every town. Carpenters made beds, tables and storage chests, potters produced a range of basic pots and dishes, while smiths shaped tools, pans and weapons from iron, copper and bronze.

The baker served his bread from a counter at the front of the shop.

Wheat was ground into flour in a mill.

The flour was mixed with yeast and water to make dough.

The bread was baked on shelves above a roaring fire.

CLEANING CLOTH

Most Romans took their woollen cloth to the fuller's workshop, where it was cleaned and treated before being made into clothes. First, the cloth was stiffened by soaking it in urine, and then it was cleaned by rubbing it with a kind of clay, known as fuller's earth. After this, the cloth was beaten, stretched and bleached. Fullers also cleaned and mended clothes for the richer townspeople.

Here you can see a fuller soaking cloth in urine.

GREAT GLASS

By the 1st century AD, the Romans had learned how to blow glass. Some glaziers made simple glass jars and sheets of glass for windows, while others produced exquisite goblets and dishes. Precious glass objects were used at grand dinner parties, or were placed in graves as funeral offerings.

Glass bowl and flask from the 1st century AD

Swirls of white glass

Ribbed glass like this was very popular.

LUXURY CRAFTS

As well as the everyday craftworkers, there were also many fine artists who specialized in luxury goods. Goldsmiths and silversmiths produced elaborate necklaces, flasks and ornaments, ivory carvers made intricate covers for writing tablets, and engravers carved delicate cameos for brooches and rings.

This cameo was carved from a gemstone called sardonyx. It shows the Emperor Tiberius.

CRAFT CLUBS

Each Roman trade and craft had its own *collegium* - a kind of social club which held regular meetings and occasional banquets. Belonging to a *collegium* was a great source of pride, and members who contributed to their club's burial fund were given a dignified funeral and an impressive tombstone.

AFTERNOONS OFF

Although the Romans worked hard at their trades and crafts, they also made sure that they enjoyed themselves. By the end of the 1st century AD, most city shops and workshops closed in the afternoon, leaving their owners free to enjoy themselves at the baths, the games or the races.

INTERNET LINKS
*For links to websites where you can take an interactive journey to Londinium and find out more about Roman trade, go to **www.usborne-quicklinks.com***

BUILDERS AND ENGINEERS

All over the Empire, Roman builders and engineers constructed vast public buildings, bridges and water systems. These magnificent structures were certainly built to last - many Roman buildings are still standing today.

INCREDIBLE CONCRETE

In the 2nd century BC, the Romans invented concrete - an amazing new building material that was strong, light and easy to use. It was made by mixing volcanic ash with water, and then adding stones to give it extra strength.

Cutaway picture of a Roman wall filled with concrete

At the top, the concrete was mixed with small, light stones.

Hollow wall built from bricks

At the base, the stones in the concrete were larger and heavier.

By filling the walls of their buildings with concrete, the Romans could build tall, strong structures that were light enough not to collapse under their own weight. These buildings were often faced with stone or marble to make them look beautiful.

ROUNDED ARCHES

Roman buildings are famous for their rounded arches - a feature that was copied from the Etruscans. These arches are surprisingly strong because each stone in an archway pushes hard against the stones next to it, which helps to hold the arch together.

Here you can see how a Roman arch was built around a wooden frame.

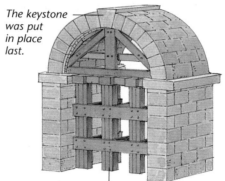

The keystone was put in place last.

The frame was removed once the arch was completed.

BUILDING BRIDGES

The Romans used arches to build huge public buildings and to construct bridges that spanned wide valleys. Building a bridge was an engineering challenge that required very careful planning.

This picture shows a simple Roman bridge being built.

VIADUCTS AND AQUEDUCTS

Some of the most stunning achievements of the Roman engineers were their multi-layered bridges, known as viaducts and aqueducts. Viaducts carried roads high above the ground, while aqueducts carried water in raised stone channels. Amazingly, some of these structures are still being used today.

Roman aqueducts formed part of a complex system of pipes and channels that delivered water from mountain springs direct to the towns and cities. Some of the Roman water systems were over 40km (25 miles) long. Because they relied entirely on gravity, the water in them had to flow downhill all the way.

1 First, the builders laid a temporary bridge across a row of boats.

2 Next, they drove a ring of wooden stakes into the river bed.

The Pont du Gard aqueduct in southern France was part of a system that carried mountain water to the city of Nîmes.

INTERNET LINKS
For links to websites where you can design your own aqueduct and find out more about Roman tools and building skills, go to **www.usborne-quicklinks.com**

WATER FOR ALL

Once the water reached a city, it was collected in huge tanks and fed through a network of lead pipes into the public fountains, toilets and baths. Only wealthy people could afford to have water piped to their homes, but some resourceful Romans attached their own illegal pipes to the public water system.

STUPENDOUS SEWERS

Roman engineers designed elaborate networks of underground drains to take away sewage and waste from their cities. The most famous Roman sewer was the *Cloaca Maxima* in Rome. It was so enormous that one city engineer made his tour of inspection by sailing a boat through it.

4 When the columns were tall enough to support the bridge, wooden frames were nailed between them.

A wooden crane was used for lifting and lowering building materials.

3 Water was pumped out of the ring of stakes, and blocks of stone were placed inside, forming a set of solid columns.

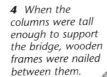

5 Once the frames were complete, wooden planks were laid over them, and the bridge was ready to use.

AMAZING ARCHITECTURE

The elegant temples of the Greeks were an inspiration to Roman architects, and the builders of the Republican period copied the Greek style closely. But by imperial times, the Romans had developed their own style of architecture, along with new building techniques. Throughout the Roman world, grand public buildings were erected to celebrate the glory of Rome.

COPYING THE GREEKS

Greek temples were rectangular in shape with an outer row of columns supporting the roof, and most early Roman temples followed this plan. But the Romans tried to make their temples grander than the Greeks', by raising them up on a platform and increasing the size of the inner room - or *cella*.

Inner room (cella)

In most Roman temples the outer columns, known as the peristyle, were attached to the cella.

USING ARCHES

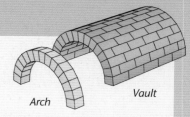
Arch   Vault

From the Etruscans, the Romans copied the rounded arch (see page 80). They used the arch for doorways and windows, and for high, curved roofs, called vaults. They also used arches as a frame to build the first circular domes.

Dome

By the 2nd century AD, the Romans had learned how to build a roof from a series of crossed vaults supported by columns. This meant that they could create huge rooms inside their basilicas and bath-houses.

Crossed vaults

The Romans copied the three types of columns used by the Greeks, but made them chunkier and more richly decorated. They also created two styles of their own - Tuscan and Composite.

Types of columns used by the Romans

Ionic (Greek)

Tuscan (Roman)

Corinthian (Greek)

Doric (Greek)

Composite (a Roman combination of Corinthian and Ionic)

The Greek Corinthian style of column, shown here, was the most popular.

BIG BUILDINGS

By using arches, domes
and vaults combined with
lightweight concrete (see
page 80), the Romans could
build huge structures that
were both light and strong.
Every Roman city had a set
of public buildings - temples,
bath-houses, basilicas and
arenas - all built on a grand
scale with massive walls and
pillars, rounded arches and
roofs, and large, airy rooms
where people could gather.

*This is the Pantheon in Rome, an
enormous temple devoted to all
the gods. Its vast dome, measuring
43m (140ft) across, was the largest
in the ancient world.*

TRIUMPHAL ARCHES

All over the Empire,
the Romans built grand
triumphal arches and set up
victory columns topped by
statues. These impressive
monuments were intended
to celebrate great Roman
victories, and their marble
sides were covered with
carvings of battles and
scenes from the glorious
history of Rome.

INTERNET LINKS
*For links to websites where you can
see amazing reconstructions of
Rome's ancient buildings and take a
photographic walking tour of Rome's
ruins today, go to*
**www.usborne-
quicklinks.com**

PAINTING AND SCULPTURE

The Romans loved to decorate their buildings with dramatic paintings and sculpture. Even quite humble homes had striking wall paintings, and Roman towns and cities were filled with larger-than-life statues of emperors, generals and gods.

A bronze sculpture of a middle-aged Roman, showing him as he really looked

ART EDUCATION

The Romans learned their love of art from the Greeks. When they first started to conquer Greece, they were amazed by all the treasures they found, and thousands of Greek carvings and statues were seized and sent back to Rome. Soon, it became fashionable to collect Greek art, and many Greek sculptors set up studios in Rome, copying earlier masterpieces and producing works of their own.

CHANGING FACES

By the time of the late Republic, sculptors had started to create realistic portraits in bronze, stone or marble. These statues were partly based on the death-masks of the Etruscans and showed people as they really were - double chins, wrinkles, warts and all.

Around the beginning of the 1st century AD, the Emperor Augustus introduced a new, idealized style for portraits of leaders, and for the next 300 years emperors and generals were shown as handsome, calm and commanding. However, ordinary people continued to be portrayed in a realistic way.

In this marble statue, the Emperor Marcus Aurelius appears noble and dignified.

SCENES IN STONE

Like the Greeks before them, the Romans carved dramatic scenes in stone and marble, but Roman sculptors concentrated on events from the glorious history of Rome. Roman carvings usually look crowded and action-packed, with lively figures set against dark, dramatic shadows.

A carved scene from Trajan's Column showing Roman soldiers in battle

By the time of the Emperor Constantine, Roman sculptors had lost much of their earlier inspiration. Although some fine work was still produced, many later Roman carvings show flattened, stumpy figures arranged in rigid ranks.

Fruit from a fresco in a Roman town house

PAINTED WALLS

Roman temples, palaces and villas were all decorated with frescoes - a kind of mural that is painted directly onto the wall while the plaster is still wet. Frescoes are very long-lasting and many Roman paintings have stayed remarkably bright and clear.

The subjects of Roman frescoes ranged from imposing arches and columns to exotic landscapes, gardens and country scenes. In temples and grand houses, artists showed gods and goddesses, while the walls of middle-class homes were often painted with scenes from daily life.

PAINTED PORTRAITS

Many Romans paid for their portraits to be painted on wooden panels or on the walls of their houses, and some Roman homes had whole galleries of ancestors. Portraits were believed to contain the spirit of the person they portrayed, and if someone was disgraced, their face would be scratched out.

This Roman portrait was found attached to a coffin in Egypt.

MAGNIFICENT MOSAICS

Roman mosaics were made from thousands of cubes of stone, marble, pottery or glass. These tiny cubes, or *tesserae*, were pressed into wet cement to make a flat, patterned surface which was very hardwearing. Many Roman mosaics still look magnificent today.

PATTERNS AND SCENES

Mosaic floors were laid in temples, palaces and villas, and their subjects ranged from simple, geometric patterns to elaborate scenes. Many mosaics depicted myths and legends, but scenes from daily life were also popular. Sometimes, a mosaic was designed for a particular room - some Roman dining rooms had a floor that looked just like a pond of tasty fish.

A mosaic of a musician beating a tambourine

This picture shows a mosaic border being laid.

The master craftsman drew up a plan for his assistants to follow.

MAKING MOSAICS

Simple mosaics were laid on site, but the more elaborate pictures were assembled in a workshop inside a wooden frame. When a picture was completed, the frame was taken to the site and set in position. Then a decorative border was laid around it.

SPECIAL EFFECTS

Creating a picture from thousands of tiny cubes is a difficult and awkward job, but Roman mosaics were often very realistic. By using a range of subtle shades, with highlights and shadows, the craftsmen really made their subjects come to life.

By the 4th century AD, Christian artists were using mosaics to decorate their churches. Some of these churches look very dramatic, with glittering figures of saints and angels covering their ceilings and walls.

This stunning mosaic ceiling was created for a church in Ravenna.

INTERNET LINKS
For links to websites where you can take a fly-through of a Roman villa and see close-ups of Roman mosaics, go to www.usborne-quicklinks.com

THE END OF THE EMPIRE

A 6th-century mosaic from Ravenna in Italy, showing
Theodora, the wife of the Byzantine Emperor Justinian

THE EMPIRE WEAKENS

For 150 years, the mighty Roman Empire seemed unbeatable, but by the mid-2nd century AD, it was showing signs of strain. The Emperor Marcus Aurelius spent most of his reign fighting off invaders, and caused widespread resentment by raising taxes to pay for the army. To make matters worse, in AD166 a terrible plague spread from the east, plunging the Empire into chaos. For the first time, people began to doubt the power of Rome.

Here, Septimius Severus is shown with his family. One of his sons, Caracalla, murdered the other, then ordered that his brother's image be removed from all pictures. You can see the smudge where his face used to be.

TROUBLED TIMES

After Marcus Aurelius died in AD180, things became much worse. His son Commodus ignored the attacks on the Empire's borders and squandered huge sums of money on public games and races. Commodus was assassinated and his successor lasted only three months before he was murdered too.

The Emperor Commodus loved to fight in the arena. He is shown here dressed as the mythical warrior Hercules.

In AD192, the Praetorian Guard sold the job of emperor to the highest bidder, but the winner was soon replaced by Septimius Severus, an army commander. Severus was an efficient emperor who defended the Empire's borders for 14 years. He was followed by three more members of his family, but each of them was assassinated, and civil war broke out in AD235.

THE ANARCHY

In the 50 years between AD235 and AD284 there was a series of over 20 emperors, most of whom were murdered. During this turbulent period - known as the Anarchy - the Empire was also struck by plague and famine. Taxes and prices rose, life got much harder for farmers and traders, and many people became outlaws to escape taxation.

Some Roman governors took advantage of the chaos to seize power for themselves. For eight years, Postumus, the governor of Lower Germany, controlled his own empire in western Europe, and set up an independent Senate in the German city of Trier.

ATTACKS ON THE EMPIRE

During the Anarchy, the Roman Empire was often under attack from Germanic tribes in the north and Sassanian Persians in the east. The lowest point came in AD260, when the Emperor Valerian was captured by the Sassanians, who later stuffed his body with straw and displayed it in one of their temples.

Sassanian warriors fought with long, heavy spears.

This scene shows Roman troops defending the Empire against Sassanian invaders.

The Roman soldiers and horses were less well protected than their opponents.

THE EMPIRE DIVIDES

In AD284, a general named Diocletian was proclaimed emperor by his troops. Realizing that the Empire was too large for him to control, he split it in two, and ruled the eastern half himself, while another general, Maximian, became emperor in the west. Each emperor chose a deputy to help him rule - the emperors took the title of "Augustus" while their deputies were known as "Caesar".

Trier

BLACK SEA

Byzantium

Rome

MEDITERRANEAN SEA

■ Western Empire
☐ Eastern Empire

Map of the Roman Empire at the time of Diocletian

Diocletian increased the size of the army by a third, and built up a mobile fighting force which could move swiftly to crush rebellions. He divided the Empire into smaller provinces and made sure that they were run efficiently. Diocletian worked hard at restoring the status of the emperor, declaring himself a god and always taking care to appear remote and godlike. He wore a pearl crown, and made visitors kneel and kiss his robe.

A NEW CAPITAL

In AD305, Diocletian and Maximian retired, and their two deputies became the new emperors. But this arrangement didn't last long, and eventually Constantine fought his way to power. Constantine reunited both halves of the Empire, but concentrated on the east. He moved the Empire's capital to Byzantium, at the entrance to the Black Sea, and renamed the city Constantinople.

THE RISE OF CHRISTIANITY

The Christian religion began when a Jew named Jesus started preaching in Judea, a small Roman province in the Middle East. After Jesus died, around AD30, his followers continued to spread his teachings, and by the end of the 1st century AD Christianity had reached as far as Rome itself.

SPREADING THE WORD

Jesus taught that people should give up their old, sinful ways, and devote their lives to God and to helping other people. The followers of Jesus believed that he had risen from the dead and hoped they would have eternal life too. These beliefs attracted many Romans, and Christianity became especially popular with poor people and slaves.

KEEPING SECRETS

Many powerful Romans were suspicious of the new religion, so most early Christians kept their faith a secret. They met in private houses, and used secret signs to show other Christians that they shared the same faith.

In this portrait of an early Christian family, there is a Christian symbol above the child's head.

In Rome, groups of Christians gathered in the catacombs - a series of tunnels under the city that were used as burial vaults. But all this secrecy only encouraged wild stories about the mysterious Christians and their strange ceremonies.

The walls of the catacombs were painted with scenes from the Bible.

PUNISHMENT AND PERSECUTION

Because the Christians believed there was only one god, they refused to worship the emperor or the state gods. This made some emperors see them as rebels.

The Emperor Nero blamed his Christian subjects for the Great Fire of Rome, claiming that they had made the gods angry, and he sent hundreds of Christians into the arena to be torn apart by wild animals.

Other emperors also had Christians arrested, tortured and killed, but the Emperor Diocletian carried out the most savage persecution. In AD303, he began executing thousands of Christians for refusing to give up their faith.

This scene shows a group of Christians being attacked by wild animals in the arena.

CONSTANTINE AND THE CHRISTIANS

In AD312, Constantine became sole ruler of the Western Roman Empire after defeating his rival for the throne at the Battle of the Milvian Bridge. Before the battle, Constantine saw a cross of light in the sky, which he believed was a sign from Christ.

Constantine was the first Roman emperor to allow Christians to worship openly. He gave Christians important jobs, paid for their churches, and made sure that his new capital at Constantinople was a Christian city. Finally, on his deathbed, Constantine was baptized as a Christian.

Part of a colossal statue of the Emperor Constantine which originally measured over 15m (50ft) high

CHRISTIANITY GROWS

About 25 years after Constantine's death, the Emperor Julian tried to bring back the state gods, but it was too late to stop the spread of Christianity. All the emperors after Julian supported the Christians, and in AD391 the Emperor Theodosius declared that Christianity was the Empire's official religion.

BISHOPS AND POPES

By the end of the 4th century AD, the leaders of the Christian Church - known as bishops - had become very powerful. They built beautiful churches and cathedrals, and sent out missionaries to teach people about Christianity. One of the most important leaders was the Bishop of Rome, who came to be known as the Pope. As the emperors grew weaker, the popes became steadily stronger.

This golden cross was a gift from a Roman emperor to an early pope.

HERMITS AND MONKS

Some of the early Christians escaped from persecution into the desert where they lived alone as hermits, devoting their lives to God. Later, these holy men gathered together to form the first monasteries. Many of these monasteries became places of learning, where monks kept the traditions of writing alive while the Roman Empire crumbled around them.

The animals were starved beforehand to make them really hungry.

The Christians faced death bravely, singing hymns and praying together.

INTERNET LINKS
For links to websites where you can find out about early Christians and see the catacombs where Christians hid, go to
www.usborne-quicklinks.com

BARBARIANS AND BYZANTINES

Ever since the second century AD, the Empire had been threatened by a group of tribes from the northeast, known as the Germani. The Romans called all these Germanic people "barbarians" and fought fiercely to keep them out of their lands. But the struggle grew much harder in AD370, when a warlike tribe called the Huns swept west from Central Asia, pushing the Germani inside the Empire itself.

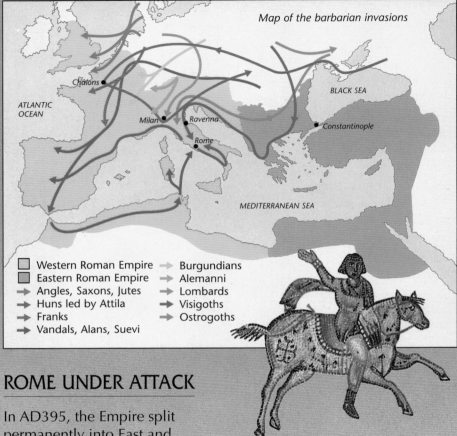

Map of the barbarian invasions

ATLANTIC OCEAN

Chalons

BLACK SEA

Milan

Ravenna

Rome

Constantinople

MEDITERRANEAN SEA

- ☐ Western Roman Empire
- ☐ Eastern Roman Empire
- → Angles, Saxons, Jutes
- → Huns led by Attila
- → Franks
- → Vandals, Alans, Suevi
- → Burgundians
- → Alemanni
- → Lombards
- → Visigoths
- → Ostrogoths

A Roman mosaic of a Vandal lord

THE BARBARIANS MOVE IN

The Romans allowed some barbarians, such as the Visigoths, to settle inside the Empire, but in return these settlers had to help fight off other tribes. Many Germanic warriors fought in the Roman army, but they kept their own commanders, and sometimes groups of barbarians rebelled against the Romans.

This eagle brooch was made by Visigoth goldsmiths, and probably dates from the 4th century AD.

ROME UNDER ATTACK

In AD395, the Empire split permanently into East and West (see map). The Empire in the east remained secure, but the Western Empire was soon overrun by barbarians. In AD401, an army of Visigoths, led by Alaric, attacked the city of Milan, where the Emperor Honorius had his palace. Honorius fled to Ravenna and set up a new capital city there.

Alaric and his warriors invaded Italy again in AD410 and attacked the city of Rome, rampaging through the streets for three days. This was a crushing blow for the Romans.

ADVANCING TRIBES

While Alaric was invading Italy, hordes of Vandals, Suevi, Alans and Burgundians were streaming into Germany and Gaul (present-day France). In AD409, the Vandals invaded Spain, and 20 years later they crossed into North Africa, one of the richest areas in the Empire. There, they set up a Vandal kingdom ruled by their leader, Gaiseric.

ATTILA THE HUN

One of the fiercest enemies of the Empire was Attila, leader of the Huns. Attila stormed through Gaul, killing thousands of people, but in AD451 he was defeated by a combined force of Romans and barbarians at the Battle of Châlons. This was the last great victory for the Romans.

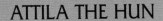

Hun archers, like the one shown here, could strike down their opponents from a distance of 100m (330ft).

INTERNET LINKS
For links to websites where you can see examples of Byzantine art, and read an eyewitness account of Attila the Hun, go to
www.usborne-quicklinks.com

THE FALL OF THE WESTERN EMPIRE

In AD455, Gaiseric and his Vandals invaded Italy and spent 12 days looting Rome. After this, the Western Empire was plunged into chaos. Powerful barbarian generals took control of the army, while the emperors in Ravenna became increasingly helpless.

The end finally came in AD476, when a Germanic general named Odoacer sent the last emperor, Romulus Augustulus, into exile. Odoacer declared himself King of Italy, and the Western Empire collapsed.

AFTER THE FALL

After the fall of Italy, the Western Empire split into lots of small barbarian kingdoms. In most of these kingdoms, people still tried to live like the Romans, but the once grand public buildings soon fell into ruins, and the Roman way of life gradually died out.

THE EMPIRE IN THE EAST

While the Western Empire was in ruins, the Eastern Empire continued for another thousand years, preserving many Roman traditions in its army, laws and government. The Empire in the east was known as the Byzantine Empire because its capital city, Constantinople, was originally called Byzantium.

A coin showing the Emperor Justinian

The high point of the Byzantine Empire came in the 6th century AD, when the Emperor Justinian won back many lands that had once been part of the Western Empire. Justinian encouraged trade and learning, and filled the city of Constantinople with spectacular churches.

This picture shows part of the city of Constantinople as it would have looked in Justinian's time.

THE LEGACY OF ROME

Although the Western Empire collapsed in AD476, the customs, ideas and inventions of the Romans continued to influence people's lives. The Catholic Church kept many Roman traditions alive, countries all over the world based their governments and laws on Ancient Roman models, and Roman buildings were copied everywhere.

ROMAN CATHOLICS

After the fall of Rome, the Catholic Church in the west continued to be controlled from Rome by the Bishop of Rome, later known as the Pope. Church services were held in Latin, and Roman learning was preserved by Christian monks who copied out ancient Latin texts.

Monks copied Latin texts and illustrated them with pictures like this.

ANCIENT FEASTS

Many Christian customs have their origins in the feasts and festivals of Rome. For example, the Christian celebration of Christmas includes some elements of the midwinter feast of *Saturnalia*, when the Romans cooked huge meals, played lively games and exchanged gifts.

EMPIRES AND REPUBLICS

Rulers throughout history have tried to recreate the glory of the Roman Empire. In AD800, Charlemagne, King of the Franks, was crowned Emperor of the Romans, and in 955 King Otto of Germany declared himself Holy Roman Emperor. The Holy Roman Empire lasted until the 1800s and had as its symbol the Roman imperial eagle.

Coat of arms of the Holy Roman Emperor

In this portrait, the French emperor Napoleon wears a golden crown based on the Roman crown of victory, made from laurel leaves.

The titles "Kaiser" and "Czar" - used by the emperors of Germany and Russia - both came from the Roman "Caesar". Napoleon Bonaparte tried to rule 19th-century France like a Roman emperor, and during the 1930s the Italian leader Mussolini attempted to create a new Roman Empire.

Some people have been inspired by the Roman Republic, rather than the Empire. In the 18th century, Republicans in France and America saw the Roman Republic as a shining example of a state without a monarch, and America today still has a Senate and senators - based on the Roman Senate at the time of the Republic.

LAW AND ORDER

In most Roman law courts, cases were tried by a judge and a jury - a type of trial that has been copied all over the world. Roman lawyers also built up a vast set of laws, and these have provided a model for the laws of many modern countries.

LIVING LIKE ROMANS

After the Empire collapsed, many buildings, roads and water systems survived, showing how the Romans once lived. For several hundred years, these structures were allowed to fall into ruin, but in the 15th century people began to copy the Roman style of building.

Today, cities and towns all over the world have grand public buildings in the Roman style, while their water and sewage systems are similar to those built by Roman engineers. People live in houses with central heating, eat fast food at snack bars, and visit public swimming pools - just as the Romans did 2,000 years ago.

The Arc de Triomphe in Paris - a 19th-century copy of a Roman triumphal arch

LASTING LATIN

The Romans had an enormous impact on the language we use today. Italian, French, Spanish, Portuguese and Romanian all come from Latin, and even the English language, which isn't so closely related to Latin, includes thousands of words that are based on Latin.

The scientific names for plants are written in Latin. This is Fuchsia fulgens, from a 19th-century guide to plants.

LETTERS AND NUMBERS

Of the 26 letters in our alphabet, 22 come from the Roman alphabet. The Romans had no W or Y, the letters I and J were both written as I, while U and V were written as V. Roman letters and numbers were mainly made from straight lines so that they were easy to carve in stone.

Latin inscriptions can be found on Roman buildings, monuments and tombs. On this gravestone for "Rinnio Novicio, mule driver", the carver wasn't able to fit the man's name onto one line.

The numbers that we use today are based on Arabic numerals which are much easier to use than Roman ones. But Roman numerals are often used on the faces of clocks and watches. (See page 107 for a guide to Roman numerals.)

A 24-hour stone clock with carved Roman numerals

WORDS AND PHRASES

Although no one speaks Latin as a first language anymore, it hasn't been forgotten. All over the world, scientists identify plants and animals by their Latin names, and some children still study Latin at school.

The English language contains several Latin phrases, such as *ad infinitum* ("to infinity") and *et cetera* ("and the rest"). It also includes many words that are based on Latin. For example, the word "urban" comes from the Latin *urbs*, meaning "city".

REMEMBERING THE GODS

Our calendar is based on the Roman system (see page 106). Some of our months take their names from Roman gods, such as Mars (March) and Juno (June), while July and August are named after Julius Caesar and the Emperor Augustus. The Romans also gave the names of their gods to the planets Jupiter, Venus, Mars, Mercury and Saturn.

FACTFINDER

The remains of a 1st-century Roman auditorium at Leptis Magna in North Africa

MORE ABOUT THE EMPIRE

On these two pages, you can discover which modern countries once belonged to the Roman Empire, and where you can go to visit Roman ruins today. You can also see a list of Roman emperors.

THE ROMAN EMPIRE TODAY

At its height, the Roman Empire covered most of Europe, and extended into Africa and Asia. Today, this area is divided into 40 different countries, from Portugal in the west to Iran in the east, and from northern Britain to southern Egypt.

ROMAN SITES

These are just a few of the places with interesting Roman remains that can still be seen today:

ITALY
Herculaneum
Ostia
Piazza Armerina
Pompeii
Ravenna
Rome
Tivoli
Verona

FRANCE
Arles
Glanum
Nîmes
Orange
Vienne

GERMANY
Saalburg
Trier

SPAIN
Alcantara
Italica
Merida
Segovia

UNITED KINGDOM
Bath
Caerleon
Chedworth Villa
Fishbourne Palace
Hadrian's Wall
Housesteads Fort
St Albans
York

TUNISIA
Dougga
El-Djem

CROATIA
Split

TURKEY
Aphrodisias
Ephesus
Side

SYRIA
Palmyra

JORDAN
Jerash

ALGERIA
Djemila
Timgad

LIBYA
Leptis Magna

This map shows which countries were once part of the Roman Empire.

▢ Roman Empire at its largest

UNITED KINGDOM · NETHERLANDS · ATLANTIC OCEAN · BELGIUM · LUXEMBOURG · GERMANY · FRANCE · SWITZERLAND · AUSTRIA · SLOVAKIA · HUNGARY · ANDORRA · SLOVENIA · CROATIA · ROMANIA · BOSNIA-HERZEGOVENA · YUGOSLAVIA · BULGARIA · SPAIN · PORTUGAL · ITALY · MACEDONIA · GREECE · ALBANIA · ARMENIA · CASPIAN SEA · AZERBAIJAN · BLACK SEA · MOROCCO · ALGERIA · MALTA · TUNISIA · MEDITERRANEAN SEA · TURKEY · CYPRUS · LEBANON · SYRIA · ISRAEL · IRAN · IRAQ · JORDAN · KUWAIT · SAUDI ARABIA · LIBYA · EGYPT · RED SEA

These Roman baths at Leptis Magna, on the coast of Libya, survived virtually intact beneath the sand dunes.

EMPERORS OF ROME

This list shows most of the emperors of Rome. A few emperors who seized power for themselves, and who ruled for only a very short time, have not been included. Some emperors appointed a co-ruler; those who ruled jointly for a time are marked with an asterisk (*).

27BC-AD14	Augustus	209-212	*Geta
AD14-37	Tiberius	211-217	*Caracalla
37-41	Gaius (Caligula)	217-218	*Macrinus
		218-222	*Elagabalus
41-54	Claudius	222-235	Severus Alexander
54-68	Nero		
68-69	Galba	235-238	Maximinus I
69	Otho	238	*Gordian I
69	Vitellius	238	*Gordian II
69-79	Vespasian	238	*Balbinus
79-81	Titus	238	*Pupienus
81-96	Domitian	238-244	Gordian III
96-98	Nerva	244-249	Philip the Arab
98-117	Trajan		
117-138	Hadrian	249-251	Trajan Decius
138-161	Antoninus Pius	251-253	*Trebonianus Gallus
161-180	*Marcus Aurelius	251-253	*Volusian
161-169	*Lucius Verus	253-260	*Valerian
180-192	Commodus	253-268	*Gallienus
193	Pertinax	268-270	Claudius II
193	*Didius Julianus	270-275	Aurelian
		275-276	Tacitus
193-194	*Pescennius Niger	276	*Florian
193-211	*Septimius Severus	276-282	*Probus
		282-283	Carus
195-197	*Clodius Albinus	283-284	*Carinus
		283-284	*Numerian
		284-286	Diocletian

WESTERN EMPIRE		EASTERN EMPIRE	
286-305	Maximian	286-305	Diocletian
305-306	Constantius I	305-311	*Galerius
306-307	*Severus II		
306-312	*Maxentius	309-313	*Maximinus II
307-324	*Constantine I	308-324	*Licinius
324-337	Constantine I *ruled both East and West*		
337-340	*Constantine II		
337-350	*Constans		
350-353	Magnentius	337-353	Constantius II
353-361	*Constantius II *ruled both East and West*		
360-363	*Julian the Apostate *ruled both East and West*		
363-364	Jovian *ruled both East and West*		
364	Valentinian I *ruled both East and West*		
364-375	*Valentinian I	364-378	Valens
367-383	*Gratian		
375-392	*Valentinian II		
392-394	Eugenius	379-394	Theodosius I
394-395	Theodosius I *ruled both East and West*		
395-423	Honorius	395-408	*Arcadius
423-425	Johannes	402-450	*Theodosius II
425-455	Valentinian III	450-457	Marcian
455-456	Avitus		
457-461	Majorian	457-474	*Leo I
461-465	Severus III		
465-467	*No emperor*		
467-472	*Anthemius	473-474	*Leo II
472	*Olybrius	474-475	Zeno
473-474	Glycerius	475-476	Basiliscus
474-475	Julius Nepos	476-491	Zeno
475-476	Romulus Augustulus	491-518	Anastasius
		518-527	Justin
		527-565	Justinian

THE ORGANIZATION OF THE ARMY

The structure of the Roman army changed a lot over the centuries. These two pages explain how the army was organized in the early days of the Republic, and later under the Empire. You can also find out about different types of soldiers and battle formations.

THE REPUBLICAN ARMY

At the start of the Republic, the army was organized very simply, and soldiers were divided into groups called centuries, each containing 100 men. Later, as the army grew, soldiers were grouped into much larger units, called legions, of about 4,200 men. Each legion was divided into groups known as maniples, containing 120 men.

THE IMPERIAL ARMY

During the Empire, the army reached the peak of its organization. It was successful because each legion was divided into lots of small, highly disciplined groups.

This diagram shows the structure of a legion in the imperial army.

CONTUBERNIUM (8 men)

A group of eight soldiers was known as a *contubernium*. The members of each *contubernium* shared a tent together when the army was on the move, and shared a pair of rooms in the army fort.

CENTURY (80 men)

Ten *contubernia* (80 men) made up a century, which was smaller than in Republican times when it had 100 men. This new, smaller century was easier to control and more effective in battle. Each century was commanded by a centurion.

COHORT (480 men)

A cohort was usually made up of six centuries (480 men), but the first cohort in every legion had ten centuries (800 men). Some of these extra men were cooks and clerks, who didn't usually fight.

LEGION (6,000 men)

A legion was made up of ten cohorts, nine of the usual size and one of 800 men, making over 5,000 soldiers in all. Each legion also included more than a hundred horseback messengers, as well as builders, engineers, doctors and a catapult maker. The Roman army had a total of 25 to 35 legions - the exact number varied over time.

TYPES OF SOLDIERS

By the time of the Empire, there were many different types of soldiers in the army. Here are some of the most common ones:

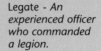

Legate - *An experienced officer who commanded a legion.*

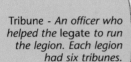

Tribune - *An officer who helped the legate to run the legion. Each legion had six tribunes.*

Praefectus Castrorum - *A senior officer in charge of the training and organization of a legion.*

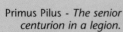

Primus Pilus - *The senior centurion in a legion.*

Centurion - *The leader of a century.*

Nine ordinary cohorts
(480 men in each)

First cohort
(800 men)

Contubernium
(8 men)

Century (80 men)

Legionary - *A foot soldier. Only Roman citizens could be legionaries.*

Auxiliary - *A non-citizen who fought in the army. Each legion had its own groups of auxiliaries.*

Aquilifer - *The standard-bearer who carried the legion's precious golden eagle during battle.*

Cornicene - *A horn-blower who sent signals during battles.*

Cavalry soldier - *A soldier who fought on horseback.*

Signifer - *A standard-bearer who carried the emblem of a century.*

THE UNSTOPPABLE TORTOISE

During the Empire, groups of soldiers advanced in a cunning formation called the *testudo*, or tortoise. The soldiers locked their shields together to form a solid barrier over their heads and around the edges of the group. This protected them from spears and arrows, and allowed the soldiers to get close to the enemy while remaining safe.

Men dressed as Roman soldiers, in the testudo formation

GODS, GODDESSES AND FESTIVALS

The Romans prayed to dozens of gods and celebrated more than 100 festivals a year. Here is a list of gods and goddesses and a brief description of the main Roman festivals.

GODS AND GODDESSES

Most of the Roman gods were borrowed from the Greeks. In this list of major Roman gods and goddesses, their Greek names are given in brackets.

Apollo *(Apollo)* - god of the Sun, music, healing and prophecy

Bacchus *(Dionysus)* - god of wine

Ceres *(Demeter)* - goddess of crops and harvests

Cupid *(Eros)* - god of love

Diana *(Artemis)* - goddess of the Moon and hunting

Dis *(Pluto)* - god of the Underworld

Flora - Roman goddess of Spring and flowers

Fortuna *(Tyche)* - goddess of good luck

Janus - Roman god of doorways and bridges

Juno *(Hera)* - queen of the gods, goddess of women and childbirth

Jupiter or **Jove** *(Zeus)* - king of the gods, god of the sky, thunder and lightning

Mars *(Ares)* - god of war

Mercury *(Hermes)* - Jupiter's messenger, god of trade and thieves

Minerva *(Athena)* - goddess of science and wisdom, crafts and war

Neptune *(Poseidon)* - god of the sea

Roma - goddess of Rome

Saturn *(Chronos)* - god of farming

Venus *(Aphrodite)* - goddess of love and beauty

Vesta *(Hestia)* - goddess of the hearth

Vulcan *(Hephaestus)* - god of blacksmiths and craftworkers

A Roman fresco showing the goddess Flora picking flowers

FESTIVALS AND FEASTS

These are some of the main festivals of the Roman year. Their names and dates are given where they are known.

January 1

After 153BC, this day marked the start of the Roman New Year. Bulls were sacrificed to Jupiter to give thanks for the god's protection in the past year, and two new consuls took up their positions as leaders of the Senate.

Early January - *Compitalia*

In the country, farmers sacrificed an animal to purify their farms for the coming year. In towns, people made sacrifices at crossroads, and then enjoyed three days of celebrations.

February 13-21 - *Parentalia*

Romans placed flowers, milk and wine on the graves of their dead parents. This was to stop the dead from feeling hungry and returning to haunt the living.

February 15 - *Lupercalia*

Two teams of young men raced around the Palatine Hill in Rome, dressed in the skins of sacrificed goats. As they ran, they whipped the spectators with strips of goatskin. It was believed that any woman touched by them would soon have a baby.

February 22 - *Caristia*

Families gathered for a meal to mark the end of *Parentalia*.

March 1

Originally the start of the Roman year, on this day the fire in the temple of Vesta in Rome was relit by the Vestal Virgins. This was also the first day of the dances of the priests. Twelve young priests danced around Rome holding sacred shields. The dancing lasted for 19 days and the dancers feasted at a different house each night.

March 15 - *Anna Perenna*

People ate picnics on the banks of the Tiber to celebrate the feast of Anna Perenna, goddess of the year. Some Romans believed that they would live for as many years as they could drink cups of wine.

March 23 - *Tubilustrium*

The sacred trumpets of war were purified in a ceremony dedicated to Mars, god of war. This was meant to bring success in battle.

April 4-10 - *Ludi Megalenses*

Games were held in praise of Cybele, the Great Mother Goddess from Turkey.

April 12-19 - *Ludi Ceriales*

Games were held for Ceres, goddess of crops and harvests.

April 21 - *Parilia*

Parilia began as a country festival when all the sheep were washed, but later it was celebrated in Rome as the city's birthday. People in Rome threw offerings onto bonfires and then danced in the flames. The celebrations ended with a large outdoor feast.

April 28-May 3 - *Floralia*

This celebration in praise of Flora, goddess of Spring, was also known as *Ludi Florales*. Tables were piled high with flowers, and people wore garlands and performed dances.

June 9 - *Vestalia*

On this day, married women visited the temple of Vesta in Rome, bringing gifts of food for the goddess. *Vestalia* was a holiday for bakers, because the Vestal Virgins baked a special bread made from salted flour.

June 24 - *Fors Fortuna*

This was a great public holiday in Rome. In the morning, people rowed down the Tiber to watch sacrifices to the goddess Fortuna, which were held just outside Rome. The rest of the day was spent picnicking and drinking.

July 6-13 - *Ludi Apollinares*

During the Republic, this festival was connected with ceremonies to the god Apollo. But by imperial times, it was just an excuse for theatrical shows, games and races.

August 13

This was the feast day of Diana, goddess of hunting. Slaves had a holiday and it was traditional for women to wash their hair.

September 5-19 - *Ludi Romani*

This 15-day festival of games, races and plays was held in praise of Jupiter. On September 13, a cow was sacrificed at Jupiter's temple and a grand banquet was held there. Statues of Jupiter, Juno and Minerva were dressed up and placed on couches so that they could share in the feast.

November 4-17 - *Ludi Plebeii*

During this 13-day celebration in praise of Jupiter, people watched plays, games and races. On November 13, there was a banquet for senators and magistrates.

Early December - *Rites of the Bona Dea*

This was a women-only festival in praise of Bona Dea, the "Good Goddess" and protector of women. Men were forbidden to attend these secret ceremonies, which may have involved dancing, drinking and the worship of sacred objects.

December 17 - *Saturnalia*

At first, *Saturnalia* lasted only one day, but later it was extended to about a week. The festival began with a sacrifice at the temple of Saturn, god of farming. People played games and gave each other gifts, and masters changed places with their slaves for a day.

LEGENDS OF ROME

Today, historians concentrate on facts, but Roman historians, such as Livy, also included many legends in their writings. These helped to shape the way the Romans saw themselves. Roman poets, such as Virgil, were also inspired by these ancient stories. On these two pages, you can read some of the myths that grew up around the early history of Rome.

TARPEIA THE TRAITRESS

While Romulus was King of Rome, the Romans kidnapped some Sabine women who lived nearby (see page 12). The Sabines were determined to seek revenge, but this was no easy task, as Rome was very well defended. The strongest place of all was the fortress on top of the steep, rocky Capitol Hill.

It so happened that the commander of the fortress had a daughter named Tarpeia, who was in love with a young Sabine man. Tarpeia agreed to open the gate of the fortress and let the Sabines in. But the Sabines were so disgusted by her betrayal of Rome - even though she had helped them - that as they entered the fortress, they crushed her to death beneath their shields. Ever after, the Romans punished traitors by hurling them off the high rock on top of the Capitol Hill. This rock was named the Tarpeian Rock, after Tarpeia the traitress.

NUMA AND THE NYMPH

Numa - the second king of Rome - was famous for his wisdom. But in fact, he was getting some help from the gods. The king had fallen in love with Egeria - one of the nymphs who served the goddess Diana. The two lovers would meet on the wooded slopes of Mount Albanus, near Rome, and when Numa had a problem, he would consult Egeria to find out the will of the gods. When Numa died, Egeria was heartbroken. As a nymph, she was immortal and could never join him in death. She wept so much that she turned into a stream that cascaded down Mount Albanus and into the Alban Lake.

THE SIBYLLINE BOOKS

In ancient times, there were several priestesses in Italy known as Sibyls. It was believed that the gods spoke through the Sibyls, solving people's problems and making prophecies. The most famous of these priestesses was the Sibyl of Cumae.

According to legend, Tarquin the Proud - the last king of Rome - was approached by the Sibyl of Cumae, who offered to sell him 12 books of prophecies about the future of Rome. Tarquin thought her price was too high, so he refused. Then, before his very eyes, she burned three of the books and offered him the remaining nine - at the same price. This happened twice more.

Finally, Tarquin was so intrigued that he bought the three surviving books - at the original price. These were the famous Sibylline Books, which were consulted by future generations whenever Rome was faced with a crisis.

MUCIUS THE LEFT-HANDED

After Tarquin the Proud was driven out of Rome, Porsena - king of the Etruscan city of Clusium - agreed to help put him back on the throne. The Etruscans advanced on Rome, but were held back by the Roman hero Horatio (see page 14). Unable to attack the city, the Etruscans besieged it instead.

A young Roman noble, named Caius Mucius, was determined to save Rome. He swam the Tiber and entered the Etruscan camp, intending to kill King Porsena. But, by mistake, he killed a secretary who was sitting next to the king. Seized by the king's bodyguards, Mucius had to think quickly. He hinted that he wasn't alone and that the king had reason to be afraid.

Porsena was furious and threatened to burn Mucius alive if he didn't explain what he meant. To prove he wasn't afraid, Mucius thrust his right hand into the fire. Porsena was so impressed by Mucius's courage that he spared his life and made peace with Rome. From then on, Mucius was known as Mucius Scaevola - or "Mucius the Left-handed".

THE STORY OF CORIOLANUS

During the early days of the Republic, Rome was at war with an Italian hill tribe called the Volsci. On one occasion, the Roman army attacked the Volscian town of Corioli and surrounded it.

While the Romans were busy besieging Corioli, they were suddenly attacked from behind by another Volscian army. At the same moment, the gates of Corioli opened and a band of Volscian soldiers rushed at the Romans head on. The situation looked grim.

A young Roman soldier named Gnaeus Marcius was on guard at the time. Marcius fought his way through the open gates of Corioli and set fire to the town. Seeing the flames, the Volscians thought the town had already been captured, and their attack faltered. The Romans won the battle and took control of Corioli. Gnaeus Marcius became a hero and was known from then on as "Coriolanus".

VIRGIL'S AENEID

The *Aeneid* - a long poem written by the poet Virgil - is one of the most famous works in Roman literature. It tells the story of the legendary Trojan hero Aeneas, his escape from the burning city of Troy, and his journey to find a new homeland. There, he was destined to start a new race of people - the Romans - who would rule the world in peace and prosperity. On the rest of this page, you can read a brief outline of the *Aeneid*.

DIDO AND AENEAS

After Aeneas and his fellow-Trojans escaped from Troy, they were shipwrecked off the coast of North Africa, near the city of Carthage. There, they were welcomed by Dido, the Carthaginian queen. As Aeneas told her about the fall of Troy and his search for a new home, she fell hopelessly in love with him. The two of them spent several happy months together, until the god Jupiter commanded Aeneas to continue his voyage.

Dido was heartbroken. Once Aeneas had gone, she called for the sword he had given her, and stabbed herself. She died cursing Aeneas and prophesying eternal hatred between his descendants and Carthage. From his ship, Aeneas could see the flames of her funeral pyre.

AENEAS IN THE UNDERWORLD

Aeneas finally reached the shores of Italy and went to see the Sibyl of Cumae. He asked her how to get to the Underworld, so he could consult his dead father about the future. She told him he had to find a golden branch to take as a gift to Proserpine, queen of the Underworld. Helped by his mother - the goddess Venus - Aeneas found the branch and hurried back with it to the Sibyl.

Then, the Sibyl led Aeneas down into the Underworld. There, they met Charon the ferryman, whose job was to take the souls of the dead across the River Styx. When he saw the golden branch, Charon agreed to ferry Aeneas and the Sibyl across the river. On the other side, they encountered the three-headed dog Cerberus, which had snakes bristling around its three necks. The Sibyl threw the dog a piece of drugged cake, which it ate greedily. Cerberus fell fast asleep, and the Sibyl and Aeneas continued their journey.

Eventually, they came to the Elysian Fields - a blissful place where the souls of the good would live forever. There, Aeneas met his dead father, who revealed the future to him and pointed out the great leaders who would make Roman history. Inspired by what he had seen, Aeneas followed the Sybil back to the world of the living.

AENEAS IN ITALY

Aeneas rejoined his friends and they sailed up the coast of Italy. When they landed at the mouth of the Tiber, Aeneas recognized this as their new homeland.

At first, the Trojans were welcomed by the local people - the Latins - but soon a long and bitter war broke out. Aeneas eventually killed the leader of the Latin army in a duel, bringing the war to an end.

The Trojans and the Latins became one people, and Aeneas married the daughter of the Latin king. It was one of their descendants - Romulus - who later founded the city of Rome (see page 11).

This mosaic shows Virgil writing the Aeneid. *On either side of him are two of the muses (goddesses of learning) who inspired him.*

DATES, TIME AND NUMBERS

The calendar we use today is based on the Roman calendar. On these two pages, you can find out about Roman months and weeks, and discover how the Romans calculated their dates. There is also information on how the Romans measured time and a quick guide to Roman numerals.

THE ROMAN CALENDAR

According to Roman legend, Romulus - the founder and first king of Rome - divided the Roman year into ten months. Here is a list of Roman months with an explanation of their names:

Martius	the month of the god Mars
Aprilis	origin uncertain
Maius	the month of Maia, mother of Mercury
Junius	the month of the goddess Juno
Quintilis	the fifth month
Sextilis	the sixth month
September	the seventh month
October	the eighth month
November	the ninth month
December	the tenth month

With this system, each year only had 304 days, so King Numa later added two new months: *Januarius* (the month of the god Janus) and *Februarius* (the month of purification). In 153BC, the start of the New Year was moved from March to January 1. But even with the two new months, each year still had only 355 days, so the Romans had to keep adding in extra days to make the calendar work.

THE JULIAN CALENDAR

During 46BC and 45BC, Julius Caesar reformed the calendar, ordering that each year should have 365 days, with an extra day every four years. This idea still survives today in our leap year. Julius Caesar's simplified system of calculating the days of the year has become known as the Julian calendar.

Finally, during the reign of the Emperor Augustus, the months of *Quintilis* and *Sextilis* were renamed *Julius* and *Augustus* after Julius Caesar and Augustus himself.

ROMAN DATES

Within each month, dates were counted from special days, known as *Kalends, Ides* and *Nones*. These special days were as follows:

Kalends - the 1st day of each month
Ides - the 15th day of March, May, July and October, and the 13th day of all the other months
Nones - the 7th day of March, May, July and October, and the 5th day of all the other months

Dates were counted back from the *Kalends, Ides* or *Nones*:

ROMAN DATE		MODERN DATE
V *Kalends Maius* =	5 days before the 1st day of May	= April 25
II *Nones October* =	2 days before the 7th day of October	= October 5

Julius Caesar, shown here, was assassinated on March 15 - the Ides *of March.*

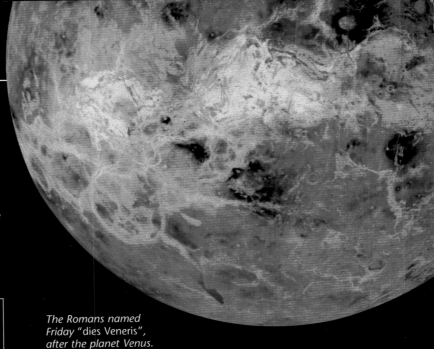

DAYS OF THE WEEK

For most of their history, the Romans didn't have a week as we understand it, though they did have a market day every eight days. Then, in AD321, the Emperor Constantine introduced a new seven-day week, with Sunday as the first day.

The Romans believed that the Sun and the Moon were planets and thought that there were seven planets altogether. The planets had been named after Roman gods and goddesses, and the days of the week were named after the seven planets:

Sunday	*dies Solis* (Sun day)
Monday	*dies Lunae* (Moon day)
Tuesday	*dies Martis* (day of Mars)
Wednesday	*dies Mercurii* (day of Mercury)
Thursday	*dies Jovis* (day of Jove or Jupiter)
Friday	*dies Veneris* (day of Venus)
Saturday	*dies Saturni* (day of Saturn)

The Romans named Friday "dies Veneris", after the planet Venus.

TELLING THE TIME

The early Romans had no way of telling the exact time of day so they had to rely on the Sun's position in the sky. Only three points in the day could be accurately known - sunrise, midday and sunset. The Romans divided the day into two parts on either side of midday, or *meridies*. The time before midday was called *ante meridiem* (a.m.), and the time after midday was *post meridiem* (p.m.) - terms that we still use today.

Sundials were set up in public squares so that people could check the time.

By the mid-3rd century BC, the Romans were using sundials to tell the time. Each day lasted as long as the daylight and was divided into 12 hours, with midday at the end of the sixth hour. The Romans didn't use minutes, and because the hours of daylight varied over the year, an hour was much longer in the summer than in the winter. The night was also divided into 12 hours, and summer nights were much shorter than winter nights.

ROMAN NUMERALS

Roman numerals are made up of a combination of the letters I, V, X, L, C, D and M. They follow a logical pattern, based on addition and subtraction. For example, 4 is written IV, meaning 1 less than 5 (V); 7 is VII, meaning 5 (V) plus 2 (II). However, this way of writing numerals meant that many numbers became extremely long. For example, the Romans needed 7 letters to write the number 78:

LXXVIII

50 + 20 + 5 + 3 = 78

GUIDE TO ROMAN NUMERALS

1	I	11	XI	25	XXV
2	II	12	XII	50	L
3	III	13	XIII	75	LXXV
4	IV	14	XIV	100	C
5	V	15	XV	200	CC
6	VI	16	XVI	500	D
7	VII	17	XVII	700	DCC
8	VIII	18	XVIII	1000	M
9	IX	19	XIX	1500	MD
10	X	20	XX	2000	MM

MONEY AND BANKING

On this page, you can find out about Roman money and banking, and also learn about some of the different weights and measures used by the Romans.

COINS OF THE REPUBLIC

In the early Republic, people didn't use money, but simply swapped - or bartered - one thing for another. As the Romans became richer and began to trade more, they needed a more precise way to pay. First, small bronze blocks were used as a kind of money, then the idea of using coins was copied from the Greeks. The first Roman coin-making factory - or mint - opened around 290BC. Soon, there were several mints in different parts of Italy.

COINS OF THE EMPIRE

When Augustus became emperor in 27BC, he declared that gold and silver coins could only be made in Rome, although the less valuable bronze and copper coins could still be made in the provinces. Eventually, the same money was used all over the Empire.

BANKERS AND MONEY-LENDERS

By the time of the Empire, the Romans controlled a huge trading network. Merchants or traders who needed money to set up businesses could borrow what they needed from money-lenders and bankers. Some money-lenders worked for the government, while others were independent and became extremely rich. Some people borrowed so much money that they couldn't pay back the loan. This meant they had to give up their homes, or even be sold as slaves.

Here are the most common Roman coins:

aureus: *gold - the most valuable Roman coin*

denarius: *silver - 25 denarii in an aureus*

sestertius: *bronze - 4 sestertii in a denarius*

dupondius: *bronze - 2 dupondii in a sestertius*

as: *copper - 2 as in a dupondius*

semi: *bronze - 2 semis in an as*

quadrans: *copper - 4 quadrans in an as*

LOSING VALUE

During the Empire, prices kept rising, so coins gradually became less and less valuable. New ones of higher value were made, but since precious metals were expensive, many new coins were made of copper and just coated with gold or silver. There were also many forged coins, and all this gradually made people suspicious of government money. Near the end of the Empire, some Romans abandoned coins altogether and went back to bartering.

MESSAGES ON MONEY

Stamping pictures on coins was one of the best ways to communicate with people all over the Empire. In imperial times, every coin showed the emperor's face on one side, and special batches of coins were made to publicize victories. When an unpopular emperor was killed, coins bearing his image were covered with scratches or taken out of use.

WEIGHTS AND MEASURES

Here are some of the most common Roman weights and measures:

The *libra* was the basis of all Roman weights, and was equivalent to about 335g (12oz).

The *pes* was used to measure length, and was equivalent to about 30cm (12in). *Pes* is Latin for "foot".

A larger unit of length was the *passus*, equivalent to about 1.5m (5ft).

The *jugerum* was a measure of area, and was equivalent to about 2,530m² (27,230ft²). It was based on the area of land that two oxen could prepare for sowing in one day.

The *modius* was the main measure of volume, used to measure goods such as salt and wheat, and was equivalent to about 9l (2gal).

ROMAN LAW

Roman law changed a lot during Rome's history. On this page, you can find out how the legal system worked under the Republic and during the time of the Empire.

THE TWELVE TABLES

In 450BC, a long list of Roman laws - called the Twelve Tables - was published. It listed laws about inheriting money, owning property, and many other aspects of daily life. Although the laws kept changing throughout the Roman period, they were always based on the Twelve Tables. One law in the Twelve Tables prevented patricians from marrying plebeians, and another gave fathers the power of life and death over their children.

REPUBLICAN LAW

During the Republic, laws were made by the Senate and the Plebeian Council (see page 21). These laws were often quite vague, so local judges had to decide how to apply them in court. When a man became a judge, he wrote a document called an edict which explained his interpretation of each law. This was usually based on the edict of the judge before him. Judges took local customs into account when writing their edict, so the laws were slightly different in each province.

If someone accused another person of committing a crime, the accuser had to summon the accused to court. If the accused refused to come, the accuser could use force to make him attend, and this often led to fights before trials.

Professional lawyers were talented speakers, or orators. This statue shows a Roman orator.

A jury of Roman citizens listened to the charges, and both the accuser and the accused had the chance to present their side of the argument. Wealthy people employed a lawyer - called an *advocatus* - to speak for them. Anyone found guilty of lying in court was executed. At the end of the trial, the jury decided whether the accused was innocent or guilty. When someone was found guilty, the judge decided what the punishment should be.

IMPERIAL LAW

At the start of the Empire, the Emperor Augustus wanted to give firmer guidelines on how to interpret laws, so he asked some leading lawyers for their opinions. Although different provinces still had different laws, all judges now had to follow the official interpretation, instead of making their own decisions. Most new laws were made by the emperor. The Senate still suggested laws, but the emperor decided whether they should be passed or not.

During the imperial period, changes were also made in the courtroom. At the start of each trial, the judge placed the accused in one of two categories: *honestiores* or *humiliores*. The *humiliores* were usually poorer, and were punished more severely if found guilty.

LAWS FOR ALL

In the 2nd century AD, the Emperor Hadrian collected all the regional edicts and made them into a single set of laws that governed all Roman citizens. If citizens living in the provinces thought they had been wrongly judged by a local court, they had the right to appeal to the legal authorities in Rome.

WHAT'S NEW?

New information on Roman life is being uncovered all the time. On these two pages, you can learn about a few recent discoveries made by archaeologists, and find out about exciting new ways of looking at the ancient world.

TREASURES OF ZEUGMA

In 2000, a team of archaeologists uncovered the remains of a buried Roman city, just before it was drowned in water from a new dam.

The city of Zeugma, in present-day Turkey, was one of the richest cities in the eastern Roman Empire. But it was destroyed by Persians in the 3rd century AD.

Experts traced the outlines of Zeugma's city walls, and explored the network of sewage tunnels underneath its streets. Among the discoveries was a lavish 14-room villa. Before leaving the site, the team rescued several mosaics, just before the city was submerged in water.

EXPLORING VINDOLANDA

For nearly 200 years, archaeologists have been excavating the site of Vindolanda, a Roman auxilary fort in northern England. Artifacts, which have been preserved in clay, reveal details about the daily life of the army and their families that lived there. The excavations still continue today.

Importantly, the discovery of private accounts and military documents, written on wooden tablets, make up the earliest written collection in British history, at over 2000 years old.

FINDS AT HERCULANEUM

The port of Herculaneum in southern Italy was destroyed at the same time as Pompeii, when Mount Vesuvius erupted in AD79 (see page 8). Recently, exciting new finds have been made at Herculaneum.

The remains of many of the victims of the eruption have been found on the beach at Herculaneum. They show that people weren't choked by ash, as experts originally thought, but died suddenly from a blast of suffocating heat. DNA and chemical analysis of teeth give an insight into the diet and health of the city's population.

SECRETS OF THE SCROLLS

During the 1750s, hundreds of burned and blackened scrolls were discovered inside a villa at Herculaneum. These scrolls contained important works of philosophy, but most of them were impossible to read.

Now, however, camera techniques developed by the NASA space team have made it possible to distinguish between the black of the charred scrolls and the black of the ink. These techniques will help experts in the future to uncover more secrets.

READING THE BONES

By studying Roman skeletons, experts known as palaeopathologists can find out about disease in Roman times. For example, they now know that while the barbarians were attacking Rome, malaria was raging through northern Italy.

Studies of Roman skeletons in Britain have revealed that some Romans living in Britain suffered from gout - a painful disease that attacks the joints. Palaeopathologists have also suggested that Roman soldiers carried leprosy from the East and introduced the disease into western Europe.

INTERNET LINKS
For links to websites where you can find out more about the latest discoveries of Roman life, go to
www.usborne-quicklinks.com

- Find out more about the discoveries at Zeugma, see photos of the amazing mosaics, and learn how archaeologists explored the site.

- Learn more about the eruption of Vesuvius and the bodies found at Herculaneum.

- Find out more about the specialized techniques scientists are using to read the damaged scrolls discovered at Herculaneum.

- Discover how archaeologists managed to reconstruct a Roman bath-house in Turkey, and look at photos of each stage of the building.

- Take a virtual tour of the Forum of Trajan in ancient Rome and see incredible 3-D architectural reconstructions and short movies about Roman life.

- Find out how Roman remains in London are excavated and processsed.

- Read about the latest archaeological discoveries.

INVESTIGATING SHIPWRECKS

The exploration of the ocean bed has led to the discovery of many lost Roman ships. Marine archaeologists dive deep underwater to investigate wrecks, climbing inside ancient vessels to take photographs and rescue treasures.

Over the past 50 years, marine archaeologists have explored Roman warships, merchant ships and barges, discovering coins, weapons, furniture and many tall terracotta jars - known as *amphorae* - that were once used to hold olive oil and wine. A few of these Roman shipwrecks held incredibly precious cargoes - statues and pillars looted from Greece by a victorious Roman army.

ROMAN RECONSTRUCTIONS

Some archaeologists try to learn more about Roman machines and buildings by reconstructing them with the same materials the Romans used. For example, experts have built full-size copies of wooden catapults, and experimented with them to see how far they can fire metal bolts.

Archaeologists have also reconstructed reaping machines and other farming equipment, and one group of experts recently recreated a Roman bath-house. These projects help us to understand how ancient technology worked, and reveal the problems Roman engineers had to overcome.

COMPUTER TECHNOLOGY

In recent years, powerful computers and the growth of the Internet have brought many important changes to the way archaeologists work. Now, experts all over the world can share their ideas, findings and photographs, combining their different discoveries to form a more complete picture of the Roman world.

Using computer graphics, archaeologists can create amazing multi-dimensional images of Roman buildings and towns, which allow viewers to go on virtual explorations inside the sites. Many can be viewed on the Internet, giving us a far more vivid understanding of how these places once looked.

This photograph shows a diver holding a Roman amphora *found at a shipwreck in the Mediterranean Sea.*

WHO'S WHO IN THE ROMAN WORLD

The next four pages give you a quick guide to some of the most famous and important people in Roman history. Names that appear in bold type also have their own entries in the guide.

AGRIPPINA (AD15-59)

Mother of **Nero**. An intelligent and ambitious woman, she prepared her son for power, and had a great influence on his decisions when he became emperor. She may even have poisoned her husband, the Emperor **Claudius**, so that Nero could take over. Nero later worried that Agrippina had too much power, and decided to have her murdered. He tried to poison her three times, and also built a special collapsing boat to drown her, but she survived all this. Finally, he had her stabbed to death.

ALARIC (?AD370-410)

King of the Visigoths, a warlike tribe from northeast Europe. He served in the Roman army under **Theodosius** but later invaded Greece and Italy, attacking Rome in AD410.

ANTONY, MARK (82-30BC)

Soldier and politician. After **Julius Caesar's** death in 44BC, he led the alliance that defeated Caesar's murderers. Then, he struggled for power with **Octavian**, until the two men agreed to divide the Empire between them. For ten years, he ruled the eastern Empire and lived with **Cleopatra**, the Egyptian queen. He was eventually defeated by Octavian at the Battle of Actium in 31BC, and soon after this battle, he and Cleopatra committed suicide.

ATTILA (?AD406-453)

King of the Huns, a warlike tribe from Central Asia. Famous for his ruthless cruelty, Attila invaded Gaul in AD451, but was defeated by a combined army of Romans and barbarians at the Battle of Châlons.

AUGUSTUS (63BC-AD14)

Emperor 27BC-AD14. The first Roman emperor, he was the great-nephew and adopted son of **Julius Caesar**. After Caesar's death, Augustus and **Mark Antony** struggled for power before agreeing to divide the Empire between them. In 31BC, Augustus defeated Mark Antony and **Cleopatra** at the Battle of Actium, and then gradually became supreme ruler of the Roman world. Originally called Octavian, he was given the military title Augustus as a mark of respect. He was a wise and fair ruler who worked closely with the Senate and brought peace after years of civil war. He also passed laws to help the poor, and built many splendid new buildings in Rome. Soon after his death, **Tiberius** declared him a god.

BOUDICCA (??-AD62)

Queen of the Iceni tribe in Britain. She led a fierce rebellion against Roman rule in AD60, and when the rebellion was defeated she poisoned herself.

BRUTUS (84-42BC)

Soldier and politician. He was a firm believer in the traditions of the Roman Republic and led the plot to murder **Caesar** in 44BC, because he thought Caesar was going to make himself king. Brutus committed suicide after losing a battle against **Mark Antony**.

CAESAR, JULIUS (c.100-44BC)

Politician, general and writer. From 58BC to 49BC, he led troops in Gaul and Illyricum, extending Roman territory as far as the English Channel. He wrote about these campaigns in seven books, called *De Bello Gallico* (The Gallic Wars). In 49BC, following disputes with **Pompey** and the Senate, Caesar returned to Italy with his army. After defeating his enemies, he became the most powerful man in Rome and was declared dictator for life. Some politicians were worried that he had grown too powerful, and in 44BC he was murdered by a group of senators, led by **Brutus**.

CALIGULA (AD12-41)

Emperor AD37-41. He was famous for his wild and cruel actions, and may have become insane following a serious illness. He grew up in the army, and was nicknamed Caligula ("little boots") because of the miniature soldier's uniform he wore as a child. His real name was Gaius.

CARACALLA (AD188-217)

Emperor AD211-217. He bribed the barbarian tribes to stay away from the Empire's borders and, in AD212, he extended Roman citizenship to all free men living in the Empire. A cruel and extravagant ruler, he was assassinated by his personal bodyguard.

CATO (234-149BC)

Politician and writer. He fought in the Second Punic War and was censor in 184BC. His book *De Agri Cultura* is the oldest existing work in Latin prose and describes the traditional Roman values of dignity and simple living that he believed in. He also wrote *Origines* - a history of the Roman people from the earliest times.

CATULLUS (c.84-c.54BC)

Poet. He wrote love poems and vivid descriptions of Roman life, and was one of the first poets to adopt the forms and style of Greek poetry. His most famous poems are those he wrote to his beloved Lesbia.

CICERO (106-43BC)

Politician, lawyer and writer. The greatest public speaker of his day, he became a famous lawyer and was consul in 63BC. While consul, he accused the senator Catiline of leading a plot against the Republic, and had several of the conspirators executed. Cicero made enemies by speaking out against important people, and he was eventually murdered by the troops of **Mark Antony**. His style of writing and speaking was imitated by scholars for centuries after his death.

CLAUDIUS (10BC-AD54)

Emperor AD41-54. After his nephew **Caligula**'s murder, Claudius was found hiding in the imperial palace and was declared emperor by the Praetorian Guards. He walked with a limp and spoke with a stutter, and although many people thought he wasn't intelligent enough to govern, he turned out to be a capable ruler. In AD43, he conquered Britain. Claudius was an excellent historian and wrote books about Roman and Etruscan history. He may have been poisoned by his wife, **Agrippina**.

CLEOPATRA (?69-30BC)

Queen of Egypt 51-30BC. A wise ruler, she was also the lover of **Julius Caesar** and later of **Mark Antony**. She joined forces with Mark Antony against **Octavian**, but they were defeated at the Battle of Actium in 31BC. Soon after the battle, she killed herself with a poisonous snake, called an asp.

CLODIUS (93-52BC)

Politician. He was born into a noble family, but got himself adopted as a plebeian, so he could be elected tribune. He led a mob of violent thugs, stirring up riots on the streets of Rome, until he was eventually killed by a rival gang. Clodius's supporters carried his body to the Senate House and used the entire building as his funeral pyre, burning it to the ground.

COMMODUS (AD161-192)

Emperor AD180-192. The son of **Marcus Aurelius**, he made peace with the barbarian tribes and spent most of his reign in Rome, living a life of extreme luxury. He loved to fight as a gladiator in the arena and was killed in a wrestling match.

CONSTANTINE (c.AD274-337)

Emperor AD307-337. The first Christian emperor, he became sole ruler of the Western Empire after defeating his rival, Maxentius, at the Milvian Bridge. He reunited the Empire and moved the capital to Byzantium, which he renamed Constantinople. In AD313, he issued the Edict of Milan, allowing Christians to worship freely.

CRASSUS (c.112-53BC)

Soldier and politician. He defeated a rebellion led by the slave Spartacus in 71BC. In 60BC, Crassus made an alliance with **Pompey** and **Caesar**, and used his extreme wealth to support Caesar's political ambitions. He was killed in battle in the East.

DIOCLETIAN (AD245-313)

Emperor AD284-305. He made radical changes to coinage, taxation, the civil service and the army. After splitting the Empire in two, he ruled the Eastern Empire while a second emperor, Maximian, ruled the West.

DOMITIAN (AD51-96)

Emperor AD81-96. He strengthened the frontiers of the Empire to protect it from barbarians, and also restored many of Rome's buildings. An efficient but tyrannical ruler, Domitian despised the Senate and persecuted many groups, including Christians and Jews. He became increasingly unpopular, and eventually his wife Domitia had him stabbed to death.

GRACCHUS, GAIUS (?160-121BC)

Soldier and politician, and brother of **Tiberius Gracchus**. He was elected tribune in 123BC and 122BC, and is best-known for introducing the corn dole in Rome, where cheap grain was handed out to the poor and unemployed. Gaius also suggested that Roman citizenship should be granted to all Rome's allies in Italy, but this was very unpopular among Romans, and in 121BC he was murdered.

GRACCHUS, TIBERIUS (?169-133BC)

Soldier and politician, and brother of **Gaius Gracchus**. He fought in the Third Punic War and took part in the destruction of Carthage. In 133BC, he was elected tribune and forced through a new law, giving land to the poor that had been illegally seized by the rich. Many senators were opposed to his ideas, and a group of them started a riot in which he was murdered.

HADRIAN (AD76-138)

Emperor AD117-138. He decided that the Empire had become too big to control, so he gave up some of Rome's lands. He also built large fortresses and walls to protect the borders of the Empire. The most famous of these is Hadrian's Wall, in northern England. An extremely cultured man, Hadrian spent lots of time visiting the provinces.

HANNIBAL (247-182BC)

Carthaginian general. He commanded the Carthaginian army against Rome in the Second Punic War. In 218BC, he led his troops across the Alps, invading Italy and defeating the Romans at Lake Trasimene and Cannae. In 202BC, he was finally defeated by Scipio at Zama, in North Africa. Hannibal later committed suicide to avoid being captured by the Romans.

HORACE (65-8BC)

Poet. He worked in Rome as a government clerk before he began writing poetry. **Augustus** later asked him to be his secretary, but he refused. However, the two men seem to have been friends. Horace's most famous works are the *Odes* - short poems on the joys of food, wine and the countryside.

JOSEPHUS (c.AD37-100)

Jewish historian and general. In AD66, he led a revolt against Roman rule in the province of Judea, but when the rebellion was crushed he joined the Romans. He then wrote a famous account of the rebellion, *History of the Jewish War*.

JULIAN (AD332-363)

Emperor AD360-363. Known as "the Apostate", he tried to restore the ancient gods almost 50 years after Christianity had been accepted. Julian cut down the numbers of his palace staff and improved the civil service, but he was unpopular because of his old-fashioned religious views.

JUVENAL (c.AD60-c.AD130)

Poet. Almost nothing is known about his life. His poems - the *Satires* - are biting attacks on corruption in Roman society, and it is thought that these poems led to Juvenal being banished from Rome for a time.

LIVIA (58BC-AD29)

Wife of **Augustus**. An aristocrat from one of Rome's most powerful families, she was wealthy and intelligent, and had a great influence on Augustus's rule. She and Augustus were married for 52 years, but had no children. After her husband's death, Livia made sure that **Tiberius** - her son by an earlier marriage - became the next emperor.

LIVY (59BC-AD17)

Historian. He spent a large part of his life in Rome writing *Ab Urbe Condita* - a vast history of the city and its people from the earliest times. It was published in instalments and made him wealthy and famous. Although this history originally consisted of 142 books, only 35 have survived.

MARCUS AURELIUS (AD121-180)

Emperor AD161-180. Most of his reign was spent at the borders of the Empire, fighting off barbarian invaders. He was an outstanding general, but also a philosopher. His journals, known as *Meditations*, show him to be a peace-loving and thoughtful man.

MARIUS (157-86BC)

General and politician. He won wars in Spain, Africa and Gaul and was consul seven times. He is best known for reorganizing the Roman army. In 88BC, tensions arose between him and Sulla, and their power struggle was one of the causes of the civil war that led to the collapse of the Republic.

MARTIAL (c.AD40-104)

Poet. He was born in Spain, but lived in Rome for many years. His short poems - the *Epigrams* - describe daily life and some of Rome's livelier characters. A lot of Martial's poetry was bitterly satirical, attacking various people for their faults, but he also wrote affectionate poems to his friends.

NERO (AD37-68)

Emperor AD54-68. He ruled well at first, but later became tyrannical, having his own wife and mother murdered, as well as anyone who dared to oppose him. He enjoyed playing the lyre and singing, and taking part in chariot races. Nero built an incredibly extravagant palace in Rome, known as the Golden House, and a myth grew up that he had deliberately started the Great Fire of Rome in AD64 to make room for his new palace.

NERVA (c.AD30-98)

Emperor AD96-98. A fair and peaceful ruler, he brought stability to the Empire after **Domitian**'s turbulent reign. Nerva also started a new tradition by choosing and adopting as his son the man he wanted to rule after him (**Trajan**).

OCTAVIAN *see* **Augustus**

ODOACER (?AD434-493)

Ruler of Italy AD476-493. Odoacer was a barbarian general who sent the last Roman Emperor, Romulus Augustulus, into exile in AD476, and then declared himself King of Italy.

OVID (43BC-AD18)

Poet. He studied to become a lawyer, but gave this up to write poetry. His work became very popular in Rome, and he was friendly with **Horace**. But in AD8, he was banished to the Black Sea by **Augustus** and never returned to Rome. His most famous work is *Metamorphoses* - 15 books of poems on myths and legends.

PLAUTUS (c.254-184BC)

Playwright. He is said to have written over 130 plays, but only 21 have survived. These are all based on Greek comedies, though they include aspects of Roman life. His works inspired many later playwrights, including Shakespeare.

PLINY (c.AD61-c.113)

Writer and lawyer. During **Trajan**'s reign, he served as a consul. Pliny published nine volumes of the letters that he exchanged with Trajan and **Tacitus**, among others. His letters contain a famous eyewitness account of the eruption of Vesuvius in AD79, in which his uncle died.

PLUTARCH (AD46-126)

Writer. He was born in Greece, but later lived in Rome, and his writings cover many different subjects, including science, literature and philosophy. His best-known work is *Plutarch's Lives* - pairs of biographies comparing Greek and Roman soldiers and statesmen.

POMPEY (106-48BC)

General and politician. He helped **Crassus** to put down the slave revolt led by Spartacus, cleared the Mediterranean Sea of pirates and won great military victories in the

Middle East. In 60BC, he joined an alliance with Crassus and **Caesar**. When the alliance broke down, Caesar returned to Rome in 49BC and seized power. Pompey was defeated and murdered in Egypt.

POPPAEA (AD??-65)

Mistress, and later wife, of **Nero**. Nero murdered his wife so he could marry Poppaea. She had a great influence on him for a while, but he is said to have kicked her to death in a fit of rage.

SCIPIO (237-183BC)

General. He led the Roman invasion of Carthage during the Second Punic War, and defeated the Carthaginian general **Hannibal** at Zama, in North Africa. After this victory, he was given the name Scipio Africanus.

SENECA (c.5BC-AD65)

Writer, philosopher and lawyer. He was born in Spain, but spent most of his life in Rome. In AD49, he became **Nero**'s tutor and adviser. He had a great influence on the early part of Nero's reign, but in AD65 he was accused of plotting against the emperor and was forced to commit suicide. His *Moral Letters* set out his ideas and beliefs.

SUETONIUS (c.AD69-140)

Historian. After a period as a lawyer, he became a government assistant to **Trajan**, **Hadrian** and others. He wrote *Lives of the Twelve Caesars* - a lively account of Roman rulers from **Caesar** to **Domitian**. As well as studying the emperors' careers, he also included masses of detail about their looks, personalities and habits.

SULLA (138-78BC)

General and politician. His first military successes were as a lieutenant to **Marius**, who later became his fiercest rival. From 88BC to 86BC, the two men were involved in a bitter power struggle. When Marius died in 86BC, Sulla seized control of Rome and made

himself dictator. He had extremely conservative views and used his position to increase the power of the Senate and the patricians.

TACITUS (c.AD55-c.116)

Historian. He served as an army officer and held several government positions, including consul. His most famous works are the *Annals* and the *Histories* - which together cover the period from **Tiberius** to **Domitian**.

TERENCE (c.195-159BC)

Playwright. He was originally a slave, but was freed by his master. He wrote six plays, all adapted from Greek comedies. Roman audiences often found Terence's plays dull, but his work was still performed in imperial times.

THEODOSIUS (?AD346-395)

Emperor AD379-395. He allowed some barbarian tribes to settle in the Empire as long as their warriors helped to fight off other tribes. For a time, he ruled both the East and the West, but after his death the Empire split permanently in two. Under Theodosius, Christianity became the official religion of the Empire.

TIBERIUS (42BC-AD37)

Emperor AD14-37. He had already retired from army life when he was called to Rome to become emperor. Tiberius was an unpopular ruler, who became frightened that people were plotting to assassinate him. He executed dozens of important Romans and fled to the island of Capri, where he stayed for the last 11 years of his rule.

TITUS (AD39-81)

Emperor AD79-81. A generous emperor, he gave money to the people of Pompeii and Herculaneum when their towns were destroyed by a volcanic eruption. He was also an outstanding military commander, capturing Jerusalem in AD70. The Arch of Titus in Rome was later built to commemorate this victory.

TRAJAN (?AD53-117)

Emperor AD98-117. One of Rome's finest military leaders, Trajan won huge areas of new land in Dacia and the Middle East, enlarging the Empire to its greatest ever extent. He built many new roads, bridges, canals and towns, and also an enormous forum in Rome, surrounded by markets, libraries and baths. Trajan's Column - a monument carved with scenes from the emperor's Dacian campaigns - still stands in Trajan's Forum today.

VESPASIAN (AD9-79)

Emperor AD69-79. He became emperor after the chaos that followed the death of **Nero**, and brought peace and stability to Rome. A strict but fair ruler, he strengthened the Empire's borders and granted citizenship to many people in the provinces. He began many ambitious building projects, including the Colosseum in Rome.

VIRGIL (70-19BC)

Poet. In 30BC, he completed a long poem called the *Georgics*, which is a celebration of life in the country. He spent the last ten years of his life writing his most famous poem - the *Aeneid* - which tells of the history of Rome in 12 books. Virgil became known as one of Rome's greatest poets, and by imperial times his works were being taught in schools.

VITRUVIUS (c.70BC-early 1st century AD)

Architect and engineer. He wrote *De Architectura* - 10 books on building styles and construction, which contain many examples drawn from Ancient Greek architecture.

ZENOBIA (3rd century AD)

Queen of Palmyra (part of the province of Syria). She led a rebellion against Roman rule, but, after several victories, was defeated and captured in AD272. Brought to Rome as a prisoner, she lived on for many years in comfort and style.

TIME CHART

This time chart outlines the major events in the history of Rome. It also shows - in smaller type, with square bullet points - important things that were happening in other parts of the world at the same time. Some of the dates have a letter "c." in front of them. This means that experts aren't sure exactly when the event happened. The "c." stands for *circa*, which means "about" in Latin.

EARLY ROME: c.1000-500BC

c.1000BC The Latin people first settle on the Palatine Hill.

- **c.1000BC** The Adena people begin building earth mounds in North America.
- **c.965-928BC** King Solomon rules Israel.
- **c.911BC** The New Assyrian Empire begins.
- **c.814BC** The Phoenicians build the city of Carthage, on the North African coast.

c.800-400BC The Etruscan civilization flourishes in central and northern Italy.

- **c.800BC** The Hindu religion spreads south in India.
- **c.800BC** The Celtic way of life spreads across western Europe.

A gold neckband, called a torc, made by a Celtic metalworker

- **776BC** The traditional date for the first Olympic Games, held at Olympia in Greece.

753BC The traditional date for the founding of Rome.

c.750BC Greeks settle on the southern coasts of Italy and Sicily.

- **c.650BC** The first coins are used in Lydia (a Greek colony in present-day Turkey).
- **605-561BC** Nebuchadnezzar II rules the Babylonian Empire, and rebuilds Babylon.

c.600BC The Etruscans take control of Rome.

- **586BC** Jerusalem is destroyed, and the Jews are taken into exile in Babylon.
- **551BC** The philosopher Confucius is born in China.

The Chinese philosopher Confucius, also known as K'ung Fu-tzu

- **c.550BC** Cyrus II of Persia founds the Persian Empire.

510 or 509BC The last Etruscan king is driven out of Rome. Rome becomes a republic.

THE ROMAN REPUBLIC: c.500-30BC

- **c.500BC** The Nok civilization begins in West Africa.

  The Nok people were gifted sculptors, and made life-size pottery heads like this.

496BC The Romans are defeated by an alliance of Latin cities at the Battle of Lake Regillus.

494BC The plebeians go on strike for the first time and threaten to set up their own city.

- **490-479BC** Wars between Greece and Persia, known as the Persian Wars.
- **c.480BC** Death of Siddhartha Gautama, the founder of Buddhism.

450BC The list of laws known as the Twelve Tables is published.

- **447-438BC** The temple known as the Parthenon is built in Athens.
- **c.400BC** The Olmec civilization comes to an end in Central America.

By **400BC** Rome is the leading city in the Latin League.

390BC Rome is attacked by an army of Gauls, and most of its buildings are destroyed.

366BC The first plebeian consul is elected.

347BC Rome begins making coins.

343-341BC The First Samnite War.

338BC Rome defeats the Latin League and takes control of Latium.

- **336BC** Alexander the Great becomes ruler of Macedonia and Greece, and begins building his empire.

Alexander the Great on his horse Bucephalus

326-304BC The Second Samnite War.

- **323BC** Alexander the Great dies. His general, Ptolemy, becomes ruler of Egypt and founds the Ptolemaic dynasty.

- **321BC** The Mauryan Empire is founded in northern India by Chandragupta Maurya.

312BC The first Roman road - the Appian Way, leading south from Rome - is begun.

- **c.300BC** The end of the Chavín civilization in South America.

- **c.300BC** The Mayan people begin building stone cities in Central America.

298-290BC The Third Samnite War.

287BC A law is passed stating that all decisions of the Plebeian Council must become law.

280-275BC The Pyrrhic Wars, between the Romans and Pyrrhus, King of Epirus in Greece.

- **272-231BC** The Buddhist emperor Asoka rules the Mauryan Empire, in India.

By 264BC The Romans dominate all of Italy.

264-241BC The First Punic War between Rome and Carthage.

- **247BC** The kingdom of Parthia is set up in Persia.

241BC Sicily becomes Rome's first overseas territory.

238BC The Romans seize Sardinia.

- **221BC** Qin Shi Huangdi becomes the first Emperor of China. The Great Wall of China is built.

218-201BC The Second Punic War.

216BC The Romans are defeated by the Carthaginians at the Battle of Cannae.

215BC Philip V of Macedonia makes an alliance with Hannibal of Carthage, angering Rome.

215-205BC The First Macedonian War between the Macedonians and the Romans.

202BC The Roman general Scipio defeats Hannibal at Zama.

- **c.200BC** The Nazca people begin making giant drawings in the deserts of Peru.

200-197BC The Second Macedonian War. Philip V is defeated by the Romans and gives up control of Greece.

149-146BC The Third Punic War, which ends with the complete destruction of Carthage.

By 146BC Rome controls all of Greece.

133BC Rome gains the province of Asia in the Middle East. Tiberius Gracchus becomes tribune.

123BC Gaius Gracchus becomes tribune and introduces the corn dole to help feed the poor in Rome.

- **c.112BC** The opening of the Silk Road linking China with the West.

111-105BC Gaius Marius defeats King Jugurtha of Numidia, in North Africa.

107BC Marius becomes consul and begins reorganizing the army.

102-101BC Marius defeats tribes of Gauls invading Roman lands.

- **c.100BC** People in Central America begin building the vast pyramid city of Teotihuacán.

91-88BC The Social War between Rome and the rest of Italy. All Italians are given Roman citizenship.

88BC Sulla marches on Rome and drives Marius out.

87BC Marius recaptures Rome, but dies the following year.

82-80BC Sulla is dictator and strengthens the power of the Senate and the patricians.

73-71BC The gladiator Spartacus leads a revolt of 90,000 slaves.

67BC Pompey clears the Mediterranean Sea of pirates.

63BC Pompey conquers four new provinces in the Middle East, including Syria and Judea.

60BC Julius Caesar forms an alliance with Pompey and Crassus.

59BC Caesar is consul.

A Roman coin showing a portrait of Julius Caesar

58-51BC Caesar conquers Gaul.

55-54BC Caesar invades Britain, but withdraws.

49BC Caesar returns to Rome and seizes power. Civil war breaks out between him and the forces of the Senate, led by Pompey.

48BC Pompey is murdered.

45BC Caesar becomes leader of the Roman world.

44BC Caesar is killed by a group of senators, led by Brutus and Cassius.

42BC Brutus and Cassius commit suicide after being defeated at the Battle of Philippi. Mark Antony and Octavian agree to divide up the Empire. Antony takes the east, and Octavian rules the west.

c.33BC Growing tension between Octavian and Mark Antony leads to civil war.

31BC Octavian defeats Antony and Cleopatra at the Battle of Actium.

30BC Egypt becomes a Roman province.

An Egyptian priest burning sweet-smelling incense

THE ROMAN EMPIRE: c.30BC-AD476

27BC Octavian becomes the first Roman emperor, and is given the title Augustus.

c.5BC Jesus Christ is born in Bethlehem, in Judea.

■ **c.AD1** The Moche civilization begins in Peru.

■ **c.AD1-100** Buddhism spreads from India throughout Asia.

AD9 Three Roman legions are massacred by Germanic tribes.

AD14 Death of Augustus.

c.AD30 Jesus Christ is crucified in Jerusalem, in Judea.

AD43 Claudius conquers Britain.

AD58-60 The Christian missionary Paul of Tarsus travels to Rome.

AD60 Boudicca, Queen of the Iceni tribe, leads a rebellion against the Romans in Britain.

AD64 The Great Fire of Rome. Nero blames the Christians for the fire, and starts persecuting them.

AD66-73 The people of Judea rebel against Roman rule.

AD68-69 The Year of the Four Emperors. Galba, Otho and Vitellius are all briefly in charge, until Vespasian seizes power.

AD70 Titus captures the city of Jerusalem, in Judea. Christianity reaches Alexandria, in Egypt.

AD73 The Roman army defeats the Jewish rebellion by capturing the last stronghold of Jewish resistance, at Masada.

AD79 The Colosseum in Rome - one of the Empire's largest arenas - is opened. Mount Vesuvius erupts, destroying the towns of Pompeii and Herculaneum on the west coast of Italy.

This is one of the many frescoes discovered in the ruins of Pompeii.

■ **c.AD100** Paper is invented in China.

■ **AD100-700** The Champa kingdom is set up in Southeast Asia.

■ **AD100-700** The kingdom of Axum, in present-day Ethiopia, flourishes.

AD101-106 Trajan invades and conquers the land of Dacia, in eastern Europe.

AD117 The Empire reaches its largest extent, after Trajan's conquests of Dacia and Parthia.

AD122-127 Hadrian's Wall is built in northern England.

AD132-135 The Romans put down a revolt in Judea. The Jewish nation comes to an end, and Jews spread out around Europe.

c.AD200 Germanic tribes attack the borders of the Empire.

■ **c.AD200-600** A civilization grows up around the city of Tiahuanaco, in Bolivia.

AD212 Roman citizenship is granted to all free men throughout the Empire.

■ **AD224** Ardashir I founds the Sassanid dynasty in Persia.

AD235-284 The Anarchy - short reigns of many emperors. Barbarians attack from the north and east. Plagues and famine sweep Europe.

AD238 A revolt against Roman rule begins in North Africa.

- **c.AD250-750** The Zapotec civilization flourishes in Mexico.

- **c.AD250-900** The Mayan civilization in Central America is at its peak.

A Mayan warrior wearing a jaguar skin and a feathered headdress

AD260 The Romans are defeated by the Persians, and the Emperor Valerian is taken prisoner.

AD268-272 Queen Zenobia of Palmyra captures Syria and parts of Egypt.

AD270 The Romans begin to abandon parts of the Empire, withdrawing from Dacia.

AD271 The Aurelian Wall is built around Rome to protect the city.

AD284 Diocletian splits the Empire into East and West.

c.AD285 The first Christian monasteries are set up in Egypt.

- **c.AD300** The leaders of the Yamato tribe become the first emperors of Japan.

AD303 Diocletian begins his campaign to persecute Christians.

- **AD304** Huns break through the Great Wall of China.

AD312 Constantine defeats Maxentius at the Battle of the Milvian Bridge, and becomes sole ruler of the Western Empire.

AD313 Constantine issues the Edict of Milan, allowing Christians to worship freely.

- **AD320** The Gupta Empire is founded in India. The Classical Age in India begins.

AD324-337 Constantine reunites the two halves of the Empire.

AD325 The First Council of the Christian Church meets in Nicaea, in present-day Turkey.

AD330 Constantine moves the Empire's capital to Byzantium, which is renamed Constantinople.

- **c.AD330** King Ezana of Axum becomes the first Christian king in Africa.

AD337-361 Julian the Apostate tries to restore the old Roman gods.

AD367 Barbarian tribes begin to set up kingdoms inside the Empire.

c.AD370 Huns invade Europe from Central Asia.

AD378 The Emperor Valens is killed by Goths at the Battle of Adrianople.

AD383 The Roman legions begin to withdraw from Britain and Gaul.

AD394-395 Theodosius reunites the Empire.

AD394 Christianity becomes the official state religion.

AD395 The Empire splits permanently into East and West.

- **c.AD400** The first towns are built south of the Sahara Desert.

- **c.AD400** Settlers from Southeast Asia reach Easter Island in the Pacific Ocean.

AD402 Goths invade Italy. Honorius moves his court to Ravenna.

AD404 The first Latin version of the Bible - known as the Vulgate - is completed.

AD409 Vandals invade Spain.

AD410 Alaric the Goth and his followers attack Rome. The Romans withdraw from Britain and Gaul.

AD429 Vandals set up a kingdom in North Africa.

- **AD430-470** Huns invade the Gupta Empire, in India.

AD449 Vortigern, King of the Britons, invites the Saxons into Britain to help him fight the Picts and the Scots. Angles and Jutes, from northern Europe, follow.

By **c.AD450** Franks settle in Gaul.

AD451 The Romans and the Franks defeat the Huns at the Battle of Châlons.

AD455 Vandals invade Italy from Africa, and destroy Rome.

AD475 Visigoths declare an independent kingdom in Spain.

AD476 Romulus Augustulus, last emperor of the West, is defeated by Odoacer, a barbarian general who declares himself King of Italy. The Empire in the West ends, but the Empire in the East continues, and is known as the Byzantine Empire.

GLOSSARY

This glossary explains some of the Roman words and specialist words that are used in the book. (If a word used in an entry has its own separate entry, it is shown in *italic type*.)

aedile A government official. Four aediles were chosen every year to be responsible for markets, streets, public buildings and public games.

amphora (plural: amphorae) A large jar with two handles, used for storing and transporting olive oil and wine.

aqueduct (1) A pipe or channel for carrying water. (2) A large bridge with a water channel along the top.

arena The central area of a stadium, where *gladiator* fights and wild-beast hunts took place.

atrium The main hall of a Roman *domus*. The central part of the atrium's ceiling was open to the sky.

auxiliary Any soldier in the Roman army who was not a Roman *citizen*.

barbarians The name the Romans gave to people who lived outside the *Empire*.

basilica A large rectangular building divided inside by two rows of columns. Basilicas were used as law courts and offices.

bulla A lucky charm worn by Roman children to protect them from evil spirits.

Byzantines People who lived in the Byzantine Empire. The Byzantine Empire was the name for the Eastern Roman Empire after the fall of the Western Empire in AD476.

cameo A miniature carving on a semi-precious stone.

Carthaginians People from the city of Carthage, in North Africa. The Carthaginians built up a powerful trading empire and fought against Rome in the *Punic Wars* from 264BC to 146BC.

catacombs A series of tunnels under the city of Rome that were used as burial vaults. The early Christians held secret meetings in the catacombs.

censor A government official, who made sure there were enough *senators* and kept the list of Roman *citizens* up-to-date. Two censors were chosen every five years and they served for 18 months.

centurion An officer in the Roman army, who led a group of soldiers called a century (between 80 and 100 men).

circus A large racetrack where chariot races were held.

citizen Originally, a man born in Rome to Roman parents, who could vote and serve in the army. In AD212, citizenship was granted to all free men in the *Empire*.

client Someone who gave political support to a wealthy man - called a *patron* - in return for help with his own career. Clients were expected to visit their patron every morning and vote for him if he entered politics.

cohort A large group of Roman soldiers. Each legion had ten cohorts. Nine of these contained six centuries (480 men) and the tenth contained eight centuries (800 men).

consul The most senior government official. Two consuls were elected every year to lead the *Senate* and command the armies.

corn dole The system of handing out free grain to the poorest *citizens* in Rome.

Curia The Senate House, where the Roman *Senate* met.

dictator A leader appointed by the *Senate* in times of crisis. He was supposed to rule for a maximum of six months and was given complete control of the army and all government officials.

domus A private house, usually occupied by one family and their *slaves*.

emperor The supreme ruler of all Roman lands. Augustus became the first emperor in 27BC.

Empire (1) All the lands that were controlled by the Romans. (2) The period from 27BC to AD476, when Rome was ruled by *emperors*.

equites A class of Roman *citizens* who were descended from Rome's first cavalry officers. They were mainly wealthy traders and bankers.

Etruscans People who lived in northwest and central Italy, whose civilization flourished between 800BC and 400BC. For part of its very early history, Rome was ruled by Etruscan kings.

forum (plural: fora) An open space in the middle of a town or city, that was used for markets, law courts and political meetings.

freedman A former *slave* who had been freed by his master.

fresco A picture painted on a wall while the plaster is still damp.

fuller A craftsman who cleaned and prepared woollen cloth before it was made into clothes. Fullers also cleaned and mended clothes for the rich.

Gauls People who lived mainly to the north and west of Italy. In 390BC, an army of Gauls attacked Rome and left the city in ruins.

gladiator A *slave* or prisoner of war who was trained to fight in the *arena* for public entertainment.

governor An official who ran a Roman *province*.

grammaticus (1) A school where boys from wealthy families could continue their education after the age of 11. (2) A teacher who taught in a grammaticus.

hypocaust A central heating system, where hot air flowed through gaps between walls and under floors.

insula An apartment block.

lararium A shrine in a private house, where small statues of the household gods were kept. Roman families held daily prayers to their household gods at the lararium.

legate (1) A senior official who governed an important *province*. (2) An officer who commanded a legion in the Roman army.

legionary A Roman *citizen* who served in the army. A group of about 5,000 legionaries was called a legion.

ludus (1) A game or entertainment. (2) A school for boys and girls aged between seven and eleven.

lyre A harp-like musical instrument.

mime A type of Roman drama performed by men and women, without theatrical masks, where the action was realistic, funny and often very rude.

mosaic A picture made from lots of small pieces of stone or glass.

paedagogus (1) A private tutor. (2) A *slave* employed by Roman parents to look after their children at school.

palla A large, rectangular shawl worn by Roman women.

pantomime A type of Roman drama, performed by men wearing masks and traditional costumes. The actors mimed the action and were accompanied by music and singing.

paterfamilias A man who was the head of a Roman family.

patrician A class of Roman *citizens* who were descended from the oldest noble families in Rome. In the early Republic, only patricians could become *senators*.

patron A wealthy Roman who helped his *clients* with their career, in return for their political support.

peristyle (1) A row of columns around a courtyard or building. (2) A garden or courtyard surrounded by a row of columns.

plebeian Any Roman *citizen* who was not a *patrician*.

praetor A government official. Eight praetors were elected every year to serve as judges in the law courts.

Praetorian Guard An important group of soldiers whose job was to protect the *emperor* and his family.

proconsul A former *consul*, who was sent as a *governor* to one of the most important *provinces*.

procurator A government official who helped to run the *Empire*. Procurators often governed minor *provinces*.

province A region of the Roman *Empire* outside Italy, that was controlled by a Roman *governor*.

provincial Any free person who lived inside Roman territory but who was not a Roman *citizen*.

Punic Wars A series of three wars fought between the Romans and the people of Carthage, in North Africa, from 264BC to 146BC.

quaestor A government official. Each year, 20 quaestors were chosen to look after Rome's financial affairs.

republic A country without a king or queen, whose rulers are elected by the people. Rome was a republic from 510BC (or 509BC) until 27BC.

rhetor A teacher who taught the art of public speaking.

Rostra The speaker's platform in the Roman Forum, which was used for official ceremonies, such as funeral speeches.

Senate The group of men who governed Rome during the Republic. The Senate still existed during the *Empire*, but lost most of its power.

senator A member of the *Senate*.

slave A person owned by someone else and used as a worker. Slaves had no rights and could be bought and sold.

SPQR Short for "**S**enatus **P**opulusque **R**omanus", which means "the Senate and people of Rome". These letters are found on many Roman coins and carvings.

stola A long robe worn by Roman women.

strigil A curved stick used for scraping oil and dirt from the skin.

terracotta A mixture of clay and sand, used to make tiles and statues.

toga A long piece of cloth draped around the body, that was worn by Roman *citizens* on official occasions.

tribune (1) An official elected by the *plebeians* to speak for them in the *Senate* and to protect their interests. (2) A senior officer in the Roman army.

triumph A victory parade through the streets of Rome.

Vestal Virgins A group of six priestesses who kept a fire burning in the temple of Vesta in Rome. They served for 30 years and weren't allowed to marry.

viaduct A bridge built to carry a road across a river or a valley.

villa A large house in the country.

INDEX

A

Ab Urbe Condita 114
abacus 47
acrobats 48
Actium, Battle of 27, 112, 113, 118
actors 70-71
Adena people 116
Adrianople, Battle of 119
advocatus 109
aedile 21, 120
Aeneas 11, 24, 77, 105
Aeneid 105, 115
Aequi 16
Aesculapius, god 76
Africa 18, 19, 23, 24, 41, 92, 97, 98, 105, 116, 117, 118, 119
Agrippina 112
Alans 92
Alaric, King of the Visigoths 92, 112, 119
Albanus, Mount 104
Alemanni 92
Alexander the Great 117
Alexandria, Egypt 118
Algeria 98
Allia, river 16
alphabets 13, 47, 96
Alps 19
amber 40
Americas 94, 116, 117, 118, 119
amphorae 41, 58, 111, 120
Amulius 11
Anarchy, the 88, 89, 118
Angles 92, 119
animals 8, 10, 40, 46, 54, 55, 56, 61, 66, 67, 68, 72, 90, 91
Anna Perenna, goddess 103
Annals 115
Antony, Mark 26-27, 112, 113, 118
apartments 30, 31, 50, 51, 59
apodyterium 64
Apollo, god 4, 102, 103
Appian Way, Italy 117

aqueducts 13, 39, 50, 51, 80, 81, 20
aquilifer 33, 101
Arc de Triomphe, Paris 95
archaeologists 6, 7, 8, 110-111
archers 33, 93
arches 13, 80, 82, 83, 95
  ~ triumphal 7, 83, 95, 115
architecture 6, 12, 82-83,115
Ardashir I, King of Persia 118
arenas 6, 8, 42, 49, 66, 83, 90, 113, 120
Armenia 36
armies 14, 16, 19, 23, 26, 32-35, 38, 75, 88, 89, 92, 93, 100-101
army, Roman 22, 23, 32-35, 36, 37, 38, 48, 75, 88, 89, 93, 100-101, 117
artists 7, 13, 79, 84-86
as (coin) 108
Asia 19, 92, 98, 112, 117, 118, 119
Asoka, Mauryan Emperor 117
asps 113
Assyria 36
Assyrian Empire, New 116
astrologers 74
Athens, Greece 47, 116
atrium 52, 53, 120
Attila, King of the Huns 93, 112
auditoriums 70, 71, 97
augurs 74
Augustulus, Romulus, Emperor 93, 99, 119
Augustus (title) 89
Augustus, Emperor
  (*see also* Octavian) 25, 27, 28, 30, 38, 39, 62, 69, 73, 84, 96, 99, 106, 108, 109, 112, 113, 114, 118
Aurelian Wall, Rome 119
aureus 108
auxiliaries 33, 101, 120
Axum, kingdom of 118, 119

B

babies 46, 103
Babylon 116
Bacchus, god 72, 102
Baiae, Italy 57
bakeries 34, 56, 78
banking 108
banquets 58, 60-61, 79, 103
barbarians 38, 92-93, 110, 112, 113, 114, 115, 118, 119, 120
barbers 63
Barca, Hamilcar 18
barracks 35
bartering 108
basilicas 30, 31, 42, 51, 82, 83, 120
bathrooms 52
baths 8, 34, 39, 49, 50, 51, 52, 56, 64-65, 76, 82, 83, 99, 111
battering rams 33
battles 16, 18, 33, 35, 74, 91, 101, 103, 113
  ~ Actium 27, 112, 113, 118
  ~ Adrianople 119
  ~ Cannae 19, 113, 117
  ~ Châlons 93, 112, 119
  ~ Lake Regillus 116
  ~ Lake Trasimene 113
  ~ Milvian Bridge 91, 113, 119
  ~ Philippi 118
beliefs 72-75, 90-91
Bethlehem, Judea 118
Bible 90, 119
birth 46
bishops 91, 94
Black Sea 89
boats 18, 26, 27, 41
bodyguards 28
Bolivia 118
Bona Dea, goddess 103
Bonaparte, Napoleon 94
bottles 13, 58, 63
Boudicca, Queen of the Iceni 37, 112, 118

bowls 7, 79
bread 58, 78
bridges 6, 14, 34, 35, 80-81
Britain 29, 36, 37, 38, 98, 110, 112, 113, 117, 118, 119
Britannicus 36
bronze 13, 33, 52, 58, 59, 84
brooches 63, 79, 92
Brutus 112, 118
Buddhism 116, 117, 118
builders 35, 80-81, 82
building sites 49
buildings 6, 7, 8, 30, 35, 50, 51, 80-83, 84
bulla 46, 47, 120
Burgundians 92
burial 35, 45, 79, 90
Byzantine Empire 93, 119
Byzantines 120
Byzantium 89, 93, 113, 119

C

Caesar (title) 89, 94
Caesar, Julius 23, 24, 26, 36, 96, 106, 112, 113, 115, 117, 118
caldarium 64
calendars 96, 106
Caligula, Emperor 28, 73, 99, 112, 113
cameos 79, 120
camps 34
canals 35
Cannae, Battle of 19, 113, 117
Capitol Hill, Rome 16, 23, 31, 104
Capri 28, 57, 115
Caracalla, Emperor 39, 64, 88, 99, 112
Caristia 103
carriages 40
Carthage and Carthaginians 18-19, 105, 113, 115, 116, 117, 120
carts 30, 34
carvings 27, 33, 38, 39, 42, 46, 55, 76, 78, 79, 84, 85, 96

Cassius 118
Castor and Pollux, temple of 30
catacombs, Rome 90, 120
catapults 27, 33, 111
cathedrals 91
Catholic Church 94
Catiline 113
Cato 19, 112
Catullus 112
cavalry 20, 33, 101
cella 82
Celtic culture 116
Celts 75
cement 52, 86
cemeteries 10
censors 21, 120
centuries 32, 100
centurions 32, 100, 120
Cerberus 105
cereals 55
ceremonies 47, 66, 75, 90, 103
Ceres, goddess 102, 103
Châlons, Battle of 93, 112, 119
chariot races 13, 68-69, 70, 114
chariots 22, 46, 68-69
Charlemagne, King of the Franks 94
Charon 105
Chavín civilization 117
chefs 61
children 44, 46-47, 48, 49, 60, 64, 72
China 41, 62, 116, 117, 118
~ Great Wall of 117, 119
chorus 70
Christianity 75, 90-91, 94, 113, 114, 115, 118, 119
Christians 6, 75, 86, 90-91, 94, 113, 118, 119
Christmas 94
churches 86, 91, 93
Cicero 15, 42, 113
Circus Maximus 68-69
circuses 68-69, 120
citizens, Roman 17, 20-21, 23, 30, 31, 32, 33, 39, 42, 49, 62, 66, 68, 78, 109, 112, 113, 117, 118, 120
civil servants 38

Claudius, Emperor 29, 36, 99, 112, 113, 118
Cleopatra, Queen of Egypt 27, 74, 112, 113
clients 44, 120
Cloaca Maxima 81
clocks 96
Clodius 113
clothes 47, 49, 62, 71, 78, 79
clowns 61
Clusium, Italy 14, 104
coaches 40
coffins 13, 85
cohorts 100, 120
coins 11, 18, 21, 24, 26, 28, 64, 93, 108, 116
collegium 79
Colosseum, Rome 66, 115, 118
columns 7, 53, 82
Commodus, Emperor 88, 99, 113
Compitalia 103
computers 111
concrete 80, 83
Confucius 116
conjurors 61
Constantine, Emperor 85, 89, 99, 107, 113, 119
Constantinople 89, 91, 93, 113, 119
consuls 21, 23, 24, 26, 103, 113, 114, 115, 116, 120
contubernium 100
cooking 49, 58-59, 94
Coriolanus 104
corn dole 31, 113, 117, 120
cornicene 101
Corsica 18
corvus 18
cotton 62
courts 30, 40, 95, 109
crafts 78-79
Crassus 23, 24, 113, 117
cremation 45
criminals 42, 66, 67, 71
Croatia 98
crops 10, 54, 55
Cupid, god 102
Curia 30, 31, 120
cutlery 60

Cybele, goddess 74, 103
Cyrus II, King of Persia 116

D
Dacia 36, 115, 118, 119
dancers 48, 66, 103
days of the week 107
De Agri Cultura 112
De Architectura 115
De Bello Gallico 112
denarius 108
dentists 77
Diana, goddess 102, 103, 104
dictators 21, 23, 24, 112, 115, 120
Dido, Queen of Carthage 105
dinner parties 48, 58, 60-61, 79
Diocletian, Emperor 89, 90, 99, 113, 119
Dis, god 102
diseases 7, 45, 76, 110
divorce 48
doctors 49, 76-77
dolls 46
domes 82, 83
Domitia 113
Domitian, Emperor 99, 113, 114, 115
domus 52-53, 120
drains 13, 50, 51, 81
drama 12, 70-71
drawbridges 18
drinking 58, 61, 103
druids 75
dupondius 108

E
eagles 33, 94, 101
earrings 63
earthenware 58, 59
Easter Island 119
Eastern Roman Empire 89, 92, 93, 113, 119
edicts 109
education 47, 48, 49
Egeria 104
Egypt 27, 31, 41, 55, 57, 69, 74, 85, 113, 115, 117, 118, 119
Elagabalus, Emperor 61, 99
elections 20, 21

elephants 18, 19, 66
Elysian Fields 105
emperors, Roman 7, 25, 27, 28-29, 30, 31, 36, 37, 40, 61, 62, 64, 66, 67, 68, 73, 74, 84, 88, 89, 90, 91, 92, 93, 99, 106, 108, 109, 112, 113, 114, 115, 118, 120
Empire, Roman 25-42, 98, 108, 109, 112, 113, 114, 115, 118, 119, 120
~ administration of 38-39
~ birth of 26-27
~ division of 89, 92, 113, 115, 119
~ end of 92-93, 119
~ expansion of 36-37
~ influence of 94-95
~ weakening of 88-89
engineers 6, 80-81, 111, 115
English Channel 24, 112
English language 96
Epigrams 114
Epirus, Greece 117
equites 20, 62, 120
estates 54-55, 56
Ethiopia 118
Etruscans 9, 12, 13, 14, 16, 17, 80, 84, 104, 113, 116, 120
executions 26, 28, 42, 44, 48, 90, 109
exercising 48, 64, 65, 76
Ezana, King of Axum 119

F
families 44-45, 46, 47, 48, 49
farming 10, 22, 54-55, 56, 111
fasces 21
fashion 62-63
feasts 60-61, 72, 94, 103
festivals 68, 70, 73, 94, 103
fire 29, 31, 34, 50, 59, 90, 114, 118
~ in temple of Vesta 30, 73, 103
firefighters 31
fish 53, 54, 59, 86
Flamen Dialis 73
Flavian Amphitheatre, Rome 66
fleets 18, 27, 41
Flora, goddess 102

Floralia 103

flowers 45, 103

folktales 11, 14

food 7, 51, 54, 55, 58-59, 60, 61, 65, 73, 103

Fors Fortuna 103

forts 34-35

Fortuna, goddess 102, 103

forum 6, 30-31, 45, 47, 51, 115, 120

Forum, Roman 21, 30-31

fountains 50, 51, 53, 56, 58

France 19, 81, 92, 94, 98

Franks 92, 94, 119

freedmen 49, 71, 120

French language 96

frescoes 7, 13, 17, 43, 52, 56, 85, 102, 120

frigidarium 65

fullers 79, 120

funerals 31, 35, 45, 66, 79

furnaces 49, 53, 65

furniture 8, 52, 111

G

Gaiseric, King of the Vandals 92, 93

Gaius *see* Caligula

Galba, Emperor 99, 118

games 46, 51, 61, 65, 94, 103

Games, the 66-67, 68, 103

gardens 53, 56, 57, 65

Gaul and Gauls 16, 17, 19, 23, 24, 92, 93, 112, 116, 117, 119, 120

Gautama, Siddhartha 116

geese 16, 46

generals 7, 18, 19, 22, 23, 24, 27, 29, 74, 84, 89, 93, 112, 113, 114, 115

geophysical surveys 7

Georgics 115

Germani (Germanic tribes) 89, 92, 118

Germany 37, 88, 92, 94, 98

gladiators 7, 8, 13, 23, 42, 49, 66-67, 70, 113, 117, 121

glass 40, 46, 53, 79, 86

goblets 7

gods and goddesses 7, 24, 28, 30, 31, 38, 44, 45, 52,

68, 70, 72-75, 76, 84, 85, 90-91, 96, 102-103, 104, 105, 107, 114

gold 13, 46, 52, 63, 64, 91, 108

Golden House, Rome 114

goldsmiths 79, 92

Goths 119

gout 110

government, Roman 13, 21, 22, 31, 38, 39, 46, 49

governors 38, 39, 88, 121

Gracchus, Gaius 22, 113, 117

Gracchus, Tiberius 22, 113, 117

graffiti 7, 50

grain 31, 40, 41, 54, 55

grammaticus 47, 121

grapes 54, 55, 72

gravestones 7, 96

Great Fire of Rome 29, 31, 90, 114, 118

Greece and Greeks 12, 13, 17, 19, 24, 47, 49, 70, 72, 77, 82, 84, 85, 102, 108, 112, 114, 115, 116, 117

Gupta Empire 119

H

Hadrian, Emperor 37, 63, 75, 109, 113, 115

Hadrian's villa, Tivoli 57

Hadrian's Wall, England 37, 118

hairdressers 48, 63

hairstyles 63

Hannibal 18-19, 113, 117

heating 31, 53, 56, 65, 95

helmets 17, 32, 33, 35, 67

herbs 59, 76

Herculaneum, Italy 110, 115, 118

Hercules 88

hermits 91

Hindu religion 116

Hippocrates 77

historians 11, 12, 14, 66, 73, 104, 114, 115

Histories 115

Holy Roman Empire 94

Honorius, Emperor 92, 99, 119

Horace 113, 114

Horatio 14, 104

horn-blowers 101

horses 39, 40, 68, 69, 89

hospitals 34, 77

houses 10, 52-53, 56, 64

Huns 92, 93, 112, 119

hypocaust 53, 65, 121

I

Iceni 37, 112, 118

identity tags 49

Ides 106

Illyricum 112

impluvium 52, 53

imports 40, 41, 55

India 41, 62, 116, 117, 119

inns 8, 40

insulae 50, 121

Internet 111

invasions 16, 18, 19, 36, 88, 89, 92, 93, 117, 118, 119

iron 33

Isis, goddess 74, 75

Israel 116

Italian language 96

Italy 8, 10, 12, 13, 16-17, 23, 24, 39, 54, 57, 92, 93, 94, 98, 105, 108, 112, 113, 114, 116, 117, 118, 119

ivory 41, 42, 79

J

Janus, god 102, 106

Japan 119

javelins 33, 35

Jerusalem 37, 115, 116, 118

Jesus Christ 42, 90, 91, 118

jewels 63

Jews 37, 75, 90, 113, 114, 116, 118

jobs 48, 49, 66, 78-79

Jordan 98

Josephus 114

Jove, god 102, 107

Judaism 75

Judea 37, 90, 114, 117, 118

judges 21, 42, 95, 109

jugerum 108

Jugurtha, King of Numidia 117

Julian, Emperor 91, 99, 114, 119

Julian calendar 106

Juno, goddess 72, 96, 102, 103, 106

Jupiter
  ~ god 72, 73, 96, 102, 103, 105, 107
  ~ priest of 73
  ~ temple of 23, 31

juries 42, 95, 109

Justinian, Byzantine Emperor 93, 99

Jutes 92, 119

Juvenal 6, 30, 47, 63, 114

K

Kalends 106

kingdoms, barbarian 93, 119

kings 11, 13, 14, 17, 93, 104, 112, 114, 116, 117, 119

kitchens 53, 58-59

L

laconicum 64

Lake Regillus, Battle of 116

Lake Trasimene, Battle of 113

lamps 8, 56

landowners 21, 22, 32, 33, 54

languages 10, 96

lararium 53, 73, 121

lares 73

Latin 6, 10, 94, 96, 112, 119

Latin League 16, 17, 116

Latins 10, 11, 12, 105, 116

Latium, Italy 10, 17, 116

laurel wreaths 22, 28

law courts 30, 40, 51, 95, 109

laws 21, 42, 48, 94, 95, 109

lawyers 42, 109, 113, 115

legates 38, 100, 121

legends 6, 11, 12, 14, 16, 86, 104-105, 114

legionaries 33-35, 101, 121

legions 33, 34, 35, 36, 37, 100

Lepidus 26

leprosy 110

Leptis Magna, Africa 97, 99

Lesbia 112

libra 108
Libya 98, 99
liquamen 59
literature 12, 47, 105, 114
Lives of the Twelve Caesars 115
Livia 48, 56, 114
Livy 6, 11, 12, 14, 104, 114
loincloths 62
Lombards 92
lucky charms 46, 74
Lucretia 14
Ludi Apollinares 103
Ludi Ceriales 103
Ludi Megalenses 103
Ludi Plebeii 103
Ludi Romani 103
ludus 47, 121
Lupercalia 103
Lydia 116
lyres 29, 31, 70, 121

M
Macedonia 19, 117
Magna Graecia 12
Maia, goddess 106
makeup 49, 63
malaria 110
maniples 100
marble 30, 40, 52, 64, 80, 83, 84, 85, 86
marbles 46
Marcius, Gnaeus 104
Marcus Aurelius, Emperor 39, 84, 88, 99, 113, 114
Marius, Gaius 23, 32, 33, 114, 115, 117
Marius's mules 33
markets 51, 54
marriage 44, 45, 46, 47, 73
Mars, god 96, 102, 103, 106, 107
Martial 6, 77, 114
Masada, Judea 37, 118
masks 70, 71
Mauryan Empire 117
Maxentius 113, 119
Maximian, Emperor 89, 99, 113
Mayan civilization 117, 119
meals 51, 58-61, 103

medicine 35, 76-77
Meditations 114
Mediterranean region 17, 18-19
Mediterranean Sea 10, 41, 114, 117
merchant ships 41
merchants 7, 20, 38, 40, 41, 51
Mercury, god 96, 102, 107
messengers 39, 100
Metamorphoses 114
Mexico 119
Middle East 23, 36, 37, 74, 75, 90, 115, 117
midwives 48
Milan, Edict of 113, 119
Milan, Italy 92
Milvian Bridge, Battle of the 91, 113, 119
mime 71, 121
Minerva, goddess 72, 102, 103
mines 42, 49
mints (coin factories) 108
missionaries 91, 118
Mithras, god 75
Moche civilization 118
modius 108
monasteries 91, 119
money 108
monks 6, 91, 94
months 106
monuments 30, 51, 69, 83, 115
Moon 102, 107
Moral Letters 115
mosaics 7, 8, 52, 56, 68, 70, 71, 86, 87, 92, 105, 110, 121
mother goddesses 74, 103
mountains 19
Mucius, Caius 104
murmillo 67
music 9, 29, 31, 45, 47, 61, 65, 66, 70, 75, 86
musical instruments 9, 31, 61, 70, 75, 86
Mussolini 94
Mutina, Italy 26
myrtle 45
myths 11, 56, 88, 104-105

N
Naples, Bay of 8, 57
NASA 110
navy 18
Nazca people 117
Nebuchadnezzar II, King of Babylon 116
necklaces 7, 63, 79
Neptune, god 28, 102
Nero, Emperor 29, 31, 90, 99, 112, 114, 118
Nerva, Emperor 29, 99, 114
Nicaea, Council of 119
Nîmes, France 81
Nok civilization 116
Nones 106
Numa, King of Rome 104, 106
numerals, Roman 96, 107
Numidia, Africa 117

O
obelisks 69
Octavian (*see also* Augustus) 26-27, 112, 118
Odes 114
Odoacer 93, 114, 119
offerings 44, 45, 72, 73, 76, 103
officials 21, 38, 40, 41, 51, 68, 69
olive oil 8, 40, 41, 55, 78
olives 54, 55
Olmec civilization 116
Olympic Games 116
omens 74
operations 77
orators 109
Origines 112
Ostia, Italy 41
Ostrogoths 92
Otho, Emperor 99, 118
Otto, King of Germany 94
Ovid 6, 68, 114
oxen 23, 54, 55

P
Pacific Ocean 119
paedagogus 47, 121
paintings 7, 9, 13, 17, 43, 49, 52, 56, 61, 84, 85, 90, 102, 110

palaces 31, 86, 114
palaeopathologists 110
palaestra 65
Palatine Hill 10, 103, 116
pallas 62, 121
Palmyra 115, 119
Pantheon, Rome 83
pantomimes 70, 121
paper, invention of 118
papyrus 46, 47
Parentalia 103
Parilia 103
Parthenon, Athens 116
Parthia 117, 118
passus 108
passwords 34
paterfamilias 44, 121
patres 20
patricians 20-21, 22, 24, 109, 117, 121
patrons 44, 121
Paul of Tarsus 118
Pax Romana 38
penates 73
pepper 41
perfume 13, 60, 63, 65
Pergamum 19
peristyles 53, 82, 121
Persia and Persians 75, 89, 110, 116, 117, 118, 119
Persian Wars 116
Peru 117, 118
pes 108
Petronius 61
pharmacists 76
Philip V, King of Macedonia 117
Philippi, Battle of 118
Phoenicians 116
Picts 119
pigments 7
pirates 10, 23, 114, 117
plague 88, 118
planets 96, 107
plants 7, 41, 45, 53, 69, 76, 96
plaster casts 8
Plautus 70, 114
plays 8, 70-71, 114, 115
playwrights 70, 114, 115

plebeians 20-21, 22, 109, 116, 117, 121

Pliny 6, 8, 57, 114

Plutarch 114

poetry 6, 65, 105, 112, 113, 114, 115

poets 6, 30, 47, 61, 63, 68, 104, 105, 112, 113, 114, 115

politicians 21, 23, 24, 47, 48, 66, 112, 113, 114, 115

pollen 7

Pompeii, Italy 7, 8, 51, 73, 110, 115, 118

Pompey 23, 24, 112, 113, 114, 115, 117, 118

Pont du Gard aqueduct, France 81

Pontifex Maximus 73

Pontus 23

popes 91, 94

Poppaea 115

Porsena, King of Clusium 104

portraits 47, 85, 90, 94

Portuguese language 96

Postumus, governor of Lower Germany 88

pottery 12, 40, 41, 58, 59, 78

Praefectus Castrorum 100

praetor 21, 121

Praetorian Guard 28, 88, 113, 121

priests and priestesses 45, 66, 68, 72, 73, 74, 75, 103

Primus Pilus 100

principia 34

prisoners 23, 48, 67

proconsuls 21, 121

procurators 38, 121

Proserpine 105

provinces, Roman 21, 36, 37, 38, 39, 40, 89, 121

provincials 20, 121

Ptolemy 117

Punic Wars 18-19, 112, 113, 117, 121

punishments 42, 47, 90

purple dye 40, 62

Pyrenees 19

Pyrrhic Wars 17, 117

Pyrrhus, King of Epirus 17, 117

Q

Qin Shi Huangdi, Emperor of China 117

quadrans 64, 108

quaestor 21, 121

R

racetracks 68-69

Ravenna, Italy 86, 87, 92, 93, 119

rebellions 23, 24, 37, 38, 112, 113, 115

religion 30, 31, 38, 45, 68, 70, 72-75, 76, 83, 90-91, 94, 96, 102-103

Remus 11

Republic, Roman 14, 15-27, 36, 44, 48, 54, 56, 58, 63, 66, 76, 82, 84, 94, 103, 104, 108, 109, 112, 114, 116, 121

~ army during 22, 23, 32, 100

~ end of 24, 26-27

~ expansion of 16-19

~ founding of 14

~ government of 21

~ influence of 94

restaurants 50, 51

retiarius 67

retirement 35

rhetor 47, 121

Rhodes, Greece 47

rings 8, 40, 44, 63

riots 21, 22, 31, 69, 113

rituals 45, 72, 74

rivers 40, 41

~ Allia 16

~ Rubicon 24

~ Styx 105

~ Tiber 10, 11, 13, 14, 41, 103, 104, 105

roads 34, 35, 38, 39, 40, 80, 95, 117

Roma, goddess 102

Romania 36

Romanian language 96

Rome 13, 14, 20, 21, 22, 23, 24, 26, 30-31, 38, 40, 41, 56, 64, 66, 68, 70, 73, 83, 84, 90, 103, 104, 105, 108, 109, 112, 113, 114, 115, 116, 117, 118, 119

~ attacked by barbarians 92-93, 119

~ attacked by Gauls 16, 116

~ founding of 10-11, 116

~ Great Fire of 29, 31, 90, 114, 118

~ growth of 12-13

Romulus 11, 104, 105, 106

Rostra 31, 121

Rubicon, river 24

rugs 52

ruins, Roman 6-7, 8, 51, 57, 65, 71, 81, 90, 97, 99, 110-111

Russia 94

S

Sabines 12, 104

sacrifices 23, 45, 72, 73, 75, 103

Saguntum, Spain 18

Sahara Desert, Africa 119

Samnites 16, 17, 67, 116, 117

sandals 60, 62

Sardinia 18, 117

Sassanians 89

Sassanid dynasty 118

Satires 114

Saturn

~ god 96, 102, 103, 107

~ temple of 31

Saturnalia 73, 94, 103

Saxons 92, 119

Sbeitla, Tunisia 6

Scaevola, Mucius 104

schools 47

scientists 77, 96

Scipio 19, 115, 117

Scots 119

scrolls 47, 110

sculptures 4, 11, 13, 17, 20, 23, 25, 27, 33, 36, 42, 48, 49, 72, 73, 74, 84-85, 91

Segesta, Sicily 12

semi 108

Senate and senators 15, 21, 22, 23, 24, 26, 27, 28, 29, 31, 38, 45, 62, 68, 88, 94, 109, 112, 113, 115, 117, 118, 121

Seneca 61, 115

senes 13

sestertius 108

Severus, Septimius, Arch of 31

Severus, Septimius, Emperor 88, 99

sewers 13, 31, 81, 95, 110

Shakespeare 24, 114

shaving 47, 63

shepherds 11, 54

shields 67, 101

ships 18, 26, 27, 31, 41

shipwrecks 7, 41, 111

shops and shopkeepers 8, 20, 30, 48, 49, 50, 51, 52, 76, 78

shrines 31, 34, 45, 52, 53, 73

Sibyl of Cumae 74, 104, 105

Sibylline Books 104

Sicily 12, 18, 116, 117

sieges 16, 33, 37

signifer 101

silk 41, 62

Silk Road 117

silver 58, 63, 108

silversmiths 79

sistrum 74

skeletons 7, 110

slaves 17, 19, 20, 22, 23, 30, 36, 42, 44, 47, 49, 51, 54, 55, 58, 59, 60, 62, 63, 65, 66, 67, 69, 71, 73, 78, 90, 103, 108, 113, 115, 121

snack bars 51, 59, 65, 95

Social War 117

soldiers (*see also* warriors) 14, 16, 18-19, 22, 23, 32-35, 72, 89, 100-101, 110

Solomon, King of Israel 116

Spain 18, 19, 23, 24, 71, 92, 98, 119

Spanish language 96

Spartacus 23, 113, 114, 117

spears 17, 66, 89

spices 41, 59

spies 34, 61

spirits 46, 72, 73, 74, 76

sport 65, 66-69

SPQR 21, 121

stadiums 66

standard-bearers 101

standards, military 32

statues 4, 7, 8, 11, 17, 20, 25, 27, 33, 36, 48, 49, 52, 53, 54, 72, 73, 75, 84, 91, 111
stolas 62, 121
streets 8, 30, 50, 51
strigil 65, 121
stylus 47
Styx, river 105
sudatorium 64
Suetonius 6, 66, 73, 115
Suevi 92
Sulla, Cornelius 23, 114, 115, 117
Sun 107
sundials 107
superstitions 74
surgeons 77
swimming pools 56, 95
swords 17, 33, 46, 67
Syria 98, 115, 117, 119

T

tablinum 53
Tabularium 31
Tacitus 6, 114, 115
Tarentum, Italy 17
Tarpeia 104
Tarpeian Rock, Rome 104
Tarquinius Superbus (Tarquin the Proud) 14, 104
taxes 20, 39, 42, 51, 88
teachers 47
temples 6, 12, 16, 23, 30, 31, 50, 51, 72, 73, 75, 76, 82, 83, 85, 86, 103
tents 34, 40
Teotihuacán, Central America 117
tepidarium 65
Terence 70, 115
terracotta 13, 111, 121
testudo 101
Theatrum Pompeii, Rome 70
Theodora, Byzantine Empress 87
Theodosius, Emperor 91, 99, 112, 115, 119
thermae 64
Thracians 67
Thurii, Italy 17
Tiahuanaco, Bolivia 118

Tiber, river 10, 11, 13, 14, 41, 103, 104, 105
Tiberius, Emperor 28, 57, 73, 79, 99, 112, 114, 115
timekeeping 107
Titus, Arch of 115
Titus, Emperor 99, 115, 118
togas 13, 47, 62, 121
toilets 50, 51, 53, 65
tombs 45
tombstones 79, 96
tools 7
tortoise formation 101
towns 6, 8, 43, 50-51
toys 45, 46
trade and traders 7, 12, 13, 18, 39, 40-41, 88, 93, 108
training, military 35, 47
Trajan, Emperor 36, 37, 99, 114, 115, 118
Trajan's Column, Rome 85, 115
travel 39, 40-41
treasure 23, 35
trials 42, 95, 109
tribunes 21, 22, 100, 121
triclinium 53
Trier, Germany 88
triumphs 22-23, 121
trochus 65
Trojans 105
Troy 11, 105
Tubilustrium 103
tunics 45, 62
Tunisia 6, 98
Turkey 19, 23, 74, 98, 110, 116, 119
tutors 49, 115
Twelve Tables 21, 109, 116

U

underwear 62
Underworld 105
urns 10, 45

V

Valens, Emperor 99, 119
Valerian, Emperor 89, 99, 119
Vandals 92, 93, 119

vaults 82, 83
Veii, Italy 16
Venus, goddess 24, 96, 102, 105, 107
Venus Cloacina, goddess 31
Vespasian, Emperor 29, 99, 115, 118
Vesta
~ goddess 73, 102, 103
~ temple of 30, 103
Vestal Virgins 30, 73, 103, 121
Vestalia 103
Vesuvius, Mount 8, 110, 114, 118
viaducts 80, 121
vigiles 31
villages 10
villas 8, 56-57, 85, 86, 110, 121
Virgil 6, 104, 105, 115
Visigoths 92, 112, 119
Vitellius, Emperor 99, 118
Vitruvius 115
volcanic eruptions 8, 110, 114, 115, 118
Volsci 16, 104
Vortigern, King of the Britons 119
voting 20, 44, 64, 66
Vulcan, god 102
Vulgate 119

W

warriors 17, 33, 39, 89, 92, 115
wars 16-17, 23, 26-27, 32, 54, 88

~ civil 23, 24, 26-27, 88, 118
~ Punic 18-19, 112, 113
~ Pyrrhic 17
warships 18, 26, 27
washing 60, 64, 65
water systems 51, 53, 80, 81, 95
weapons 17, 23, 32, 33, 35, 67
weddings 44, 45, 73
weights and measures 108
Western Roman Empire 89, 92, 93, 113, 119
wild-beast hunts 66, 67
windows 53
wine 8, 12, 40, 41, 55, 58, 72, 73, 76, 77, 103
women 12, 20, 47, 48, 58, 66, 71, 72, 74, 76, 78
workshops 8, 35, 78, 86
World Wide Web 111
wrestling 113
writers 6, 8, 10, 11, 12, 14, 30, 41, 42, 47, 48, 57, 61, 63, 66, 68, 70, 73, 77, 104, 105, 112, 113, 114, 115
writing 6, 47, 91

XYZ

Yamato tribe 119
Zama, Africa 19, 113, 115, 117
Zapotec civilization 119
Zenobia, Queen of Palmyra 115, 119
Zeugma 110
Zeus, god 72, 102

BC and AD

Most of the dates in this book have the letters **BC** or **AD** next to them.

• **BC** stands for "before Christ". BC dates are counted back from the birth of Christ, so 300BC means 300 years before the birth of Christ.

• **AD** is used with dates after the birth of Christ, such as AD50. It stands for *Anno Domini*, which is Latin for "in the year of the Lord".

ACKNOWLEDGEMENTS

Every effort has been made to trace the copyright holders of material in this book. If any rights have been omitted, the publishers offer their sincere apologies and will rectify this in any subsequent editions, following notification. The publishers are grateful to the following individuals and organizations for their permission to reproduce material on the following pages (t = top, m = middle, b = bottom, l = left, r = right):

front cover (statue) ©akg-images, (mosaic) ©Leemage/Corbis; **end papers** ©James L. Amos/CORBIS; **title page** ©Mimmo Jodice/CORBIS; **p2** ©Araldo de Luca/CORBIS; **p4** (bl) ©Mimmo Jodice/CORBIS, (background) ©Digital Vision; **p6** ©Christine Osborne/CORBIS; **p7** (t) ©Archivo Iconografico, S. A./CORBIS, (m) ©Roger Wood/CORBIS, (br) David Scharf/Science Photo Library; **p8** ©Roger Ressmeyer/CORBIS; **p9** The Art Archive/Dagli Orti; **p12** ©Jonathan Blair/CORBIS; **p13** (l) ©Copyright The British Museum, (r) ©Araldo de Luca/CORBIS; **p15** AKG Photo; **p17** (t) ©Archivo Iconografico, S. A./CORBIS, (br) ©Mimmo Jodice/CORBIS; **p20** (bl) Villa dei Misteri, Pompeii, Italy/Bridgeman Art Library, (r) ©Gianni Dagli Orti/CORBIS; **p23** ©Archivo Iconografico, S. A./CORBIS; **p24** ©Donald Cooper PHOTOSTAGE; **p25** ©Araldo de Luca/CORBIS; **p27** Photo Scala, Florence; **p28** (m) ©BBC Picture Archives, (tr) ©Araldo de Luca/CORBIS; **p29** (tl) ©Archivo Iconografico, S. A./CORBIS, (br) ©Copyright The British Museum; **p32** © Charles & Josette Lenars/CORBIS; **p33** (t) ©Copyright The British Museum, (bl) AKG London/Erich Lessing, (br) ©Araldo de Luca/CORBIS; **p35** ©Copyright The British Museum; **p36** ©Archivo Iconografico, S. A./ CORBIS; **p37** (t) ©Historical Picture Archive/CORBIS, (b) ©Robert Estall/CORBIS; **p38** ©Kevin Schafer/CORBIS; **p39** (t) Photo Scala, Florence, (b) ©Araldo de Luca/CORBIS; **p40** ©Elio Ciol/CORBIS; **p42** ©Araldo de Luca/CORBIS; **p43** Metropolitan Museum of Art, New York, USA/Bridgeman Art Library; **p44** (m) ©Copyright The British Museum, (b) The Art Archive/Museo Civico Trieste/Dagli Orti (A); **p45** ©Copyright The British Museum; **p46** (ml) ©Archivo Iconografico, S. A./CORBIS, (tr) ©Copyright The British Museum, (b) AKG London/Erich Lessing; **p47** Photo Scala, Florence; **p48** (bl) ©Araldo de Luca/CORBIS; **pp48-49** Photo Scala, Florence; **p51** ©Roger Ressmeyer/CORBIS; **p52** Château de Versailles, France/Peter Willi/Bridgeman Art Library; **p54** ©Copyright The British Museum; **p55** (tm) ©Craig Lovell/CORBIS, (tr) ©Archivo Iconografico, S. A./CORBIS; **p56** (background) ©Araldo de Luca/CORBIS, (bl) The Art Archive/Archaeological Museum, Naples/Dagli Orti (A), (tr) ©Mimmo Jodice/CORBIS; **p57** ©Roger Wood/CORBIS; **p58** ©Mimmo Jodice/CORBIS; **p61** (t) ©Mimmo Jodice/CORBIS, (b) Private Collection/Bridgeman Art Library; **p62** (background) ©Mimmo Jodice/CORBIS, (m) Louvre, Paris, France/Peter Willi/Bridgeman Art Library; **p63** © Araldo de Luca/CORBIS; **p65** ©Roger Wood/CORBIS; **p67** ©Ruggero Vanni/CORBIS; **p68** ©Araldo de Luca/CORBIS; **p70** ©Archivo Iconografico, S. A./CORBIS; **p71** (t) Photo Scala, Florence, (b) ©Adam Woolfitt/CORBIS; **p72** (tl) ©Digital Vision, (bl) ©Mimmo Jodice/CORBIS; **p73** (l) The Art Archive/Archaeological Museum, Naples/Dagli Orti (A), (tr) ©Arte & Immagini srl/ CORBIS, (br) ©Mimmo Jodice/CORBIS; **p75** Photo Scala, Florence; **p76** ©Araldo de Luca/CORBIS; **p77** Photo Scala, Florence; **p78** Photo Scala, Florence; **p79** (b) Kunsthistorisches Museum, Vienna, Austria/Bridgeman Art Library, (tr) ©Michael Holford; **p81** ©Ric Ergenbright/CORBIS; **p82** ©Eric and David Hosking/CORBIS; **p83** ©Bill Ross/CORBIS; p84 (b) ©Archivo Iconografico, S. A./CORBIS, (tr) Werner Forman Archive/Museo Archeologico Nazionale, Naples; **p85** (l) ©Vittoriano Rastelli/CORBIS, (tr) Photo Scala, Florence, (br) ©Roger Wood/CORBIS; **p86** (m) The Art Archive/Archaeological Museum, Naples/Dagli Orti (A), (br) Battistero Neoniano, Ravenna, Italy/Bridgeman Art Library; **p87** The Art Archive/Dagli Orti (A); **p88** (bl) ©Araldo de Luca/CORBIS, (tr) Staatliche Museen, Berlin, Germany/Bridgeman Art Library; **p90** ©Archivo Iconografico, S. A./CORBIS; **p91** ©Araldo de Luca/CORBIS; **p94** (bl) ©Historical Picture Archive/CORBIS, (tr) The Art Archive/Musée de Versailles/Dagli Orti; **p95** ©Vince Streano/CORBIS; **p96** (background) ©Historical Picture Archive/CORBIS, (bl) ©Royalty-Free/CORBIS, (m) ©Archivo Iconografico, S. A./CORBIS, (tr) ©2001 The Natural History Museum, London; **p97** ©Roger Wood/CORBIS; **p99** ©Roger Wood/CORBIS; **p101** ©Charles & Josette Lenars/CORBIS; **p102** ©Mimmo Jodice/CORBIS; **p105** ©Roger Wood/CORBIS; **p107** ©Digital Vision; **p109** ©Archivo Iconografico, S. A./CORBIS; **p111** ©Jeffrey L. Rotman/CORBIS.